real food
for kids

real food
for kids

quick recipes for healthy children

RACHAEL ANNE HILL

PHOTOGRAPHY BY NOEL MURPHY

RYLAND
PETERS
& SMALL

LONDON NEW YORK

Senior Designer Anna Murphy
Editor Sharon Cochrane
Picture Research Tracy Ogino
Production Patricia Harrington
Art Director Gabriella Le Grazie
Publishing Director Alison Starling

Food Stylist Joss Herd
Assistant Food Stylist Harry Eastwood
Stylist Chloe Brown
Recipe Development and Testing Gina Steer
Index Hilary Bird

First published in Great Britain in 2005 by Ryland Peters & Small
20–21 Jockey's Fields
London WC1R 4BW
www.rylandpeters.com

10 9 8 7 6 5 4 3 2 1

ISBN 1 84172 813 6

A catalogue record for this book is available from the British Library.

Printed in China

Notes

All spoon measurements are level unless otherwise
specified.

Ovens should be preheated to the specified
temperature. If using a fan-assisted oven, cooking
times should be reduced according to the
manufacturer's instructions.

All eggs are medium unless otherwise specified.
I recommend using free-range, organic eggs where
possible. Uncooked or partly cooked eggs should
not be served to the very young, the very old,
those with compromised immune systems, or to
pregnant women.

All fruit and vegetables should be washed thoroughly.

Whole nuts should not be served to children under
the age of five because of the risk of choking.
Always chop nuts or grind them finely.

Honey should not be served to children under
12 months of age.

To sterilize preserving jars, wash them in hot, soapy
water and rinse in boiling water. Place them in a
large saucepan and cover with hot water. With the
saucepan lid on, bring the water to the boil and
continue boiling for 15 minutes. Turn off the heat,
leaving the jars in the hot water until just before they
are to be filled. Drain and dry the jars. Sterilize the
lids by boiling them for 5 minutes or according to the
manufacturer's instructions. Jars should be filled and
sealed while they are still hot.

CONTENTS

6   YOUR CHILD'S DIET

     8   WHAT'S THE PROBLEM?

     10   WHAT YOUR CHILDREN NEED FOR
           GOOD HEALTH

     14   WHAT KIDS SHOULD AVOID

     20   THE SOLUTION

     26   YOUR KITCHEN

28   RECIPES

     30   BREAKFAST

     44   LUNCH BOXES, SNACKS & DRINKS

     72   LUNCHES & SUPPERS

     114   PUDDINGS

     130   PARTY FOOD

142   INDEX

144   ACKNOWLEDGMENTS

YOUR CHILD'S DIET

WHAT'S THE PROBLEM?

All parents want the best for their children and naturally want them to be fit and healthy. The building blocks of good health begin with a nutritious, balanced diet, so no parent would intentionally feed their child unhealthy foods and yet, according to recent government figures:

92% of children have intakes of saturated fat that exceed the maximum recommended level for adults

83% of children eat more added sugars than the maximum recommended level for adults

the average child eats **less than half** the recommended amount of fruit and vegetables per day

over 50% of all children eat twice as much salt as they should

the average child eats **over 80** food additives a day

WHY ARE KIDS EATING SUCH UNHEALTHY DIETS?

Over the past 20 to 30 years, freshly prepared, home-cooked food has gradually been replaced by commercial, ready-made alternatives. So much so that large numbers of children today are eating a diet that consists almost entirely of foods that have been prepared outside the home – from breakfast cereals and snacks to their evening meal. While there is no denying the convenience of feeding our children in this way, the fact remains that the companies preparing these foods are primarily in business to create healthy profits, not healthy children.

In theory, these two objectives are not mutually exclusive, but a closer inspection of the vast majority of commercially prepared foods, especially those targeted specifically at children, shows that they are rarely achieved in tandem. Most of these foods are made from poor-quality ingredients, are low in nutrients, high in saturated fat, salt and sugar, bulked out with cheap fillers, coloured, flavoured to mask poor taste and full of preservatives.

A recent survey of over 400 so-called 'child-friendly' foods found evidence of very high levels of fat, salt and sugar. They were also shown to contain an average of five additives – with some as many as 16 – some of which are known to cause temper tantrums, lack of concentration, excessive fidgeting, interrupting, hyperactivity, an inability to sleep and bed wetting in 25 per cent of all young children. More than one-third of the products contained colourings, including Azo dyes – known to be linked to hyperactivity, asthma attacks and rashes, while over 75 per cent had flavourings, including monosodium glutamate, guanosine and sodium 5'-ribonucleotide, that can cause rashes, lack of concentration and hyperactivity.

DON'T BELIEVE THE HYPE

The true nutritional quality of foods marketed specifically at children is all too often hidden behind poorly labelled, brightly coloured packaging and reassuring – but often highly misleading – health claims. Millions of pounds are spent on television advertisements for these products, strategically placed between both our own and our kids' favourite shows, with the intention of convincing us that these products are healthier, tastier and more desirable than they really are.

So successful has this marketing been that almost every kitchen is stocked full of ready-prepared food. Likewise, kids' lunch boxes are packed with crisps, sweets, sugar-laden cakes and highly processed, 'child-friendly' snacks – many of which are so nutritionally inferior they should carry a health warning.

COSTLY CONVENIENCE

In the last ten years alone, childhood obesity has increased by 300 per cent. Incidences of cancer are also increasing year on year, heart disease is our biggest killer and type 2 diabetes – a disease traditionally only associated with adults – is now appearing in children as young as 12 years of age. A poor diet has been a large contributing factor towards these worrying statistics. In fact, the health consequences of eating a diet made up predominantly of nutritionally inferior foods are so profound that in the USA there have been cases where children are even failing to outlive their parents.

READY MEALS

With parents becoming busier and more ready meals and snacks appearing on the supermarket shelves, increasing numbers of children are hardly ever given the opportunity to eat home-cooked food made from fresh ingredients. On the rare occasions that they are given such food, their taste buds are so accustomed to the high fat, salt and sugar content of the commercially prepared foods that they invariably reject it. This only serves to confirm our belief that kids actually 'need' to eat over-processed, nutritionally inferior foods – a belief that has become so ingrained that our kids are routinely fed these foods not only by ourselves but by nurseries, schools and restaurants, too. This is why it is important to keep the amount of commercially prepared foods our children eat to a minimum right from day one, which means weaning babies on home-cooked foods rather than on the often bland, artificial tasting, shop-bought jars.

This isn't to say that children can't be coaxed away from highly processed foods, it may just take a little longer. That's why this book is packed with all the kids' favourites. The difference is that not only will the burgers, fish fingers and chicken nuggets you make taste a whole lot better than anything you can buy, they will also be far higher in protein, vitamins and minerals, much lower in fat and salt and totally additive-free. Also, when your children experience how good a real burger can taste, getting them to eat a healthier diet might be easier than you anticipated.

Did You Know?
Young people today consume 25 times more confectionery and 30 times more soft drinks than they did 50 years ago.

WHAT YOUR CHILDREN NEED FOR GOOD HEALTH

In order for children to get all the nutrients they need for healthy growth and development, they need a nutritious balanced diet. The easiest way to guarantee your children are getting all the nutrients they need is to provide as varied a diet as possible, based roughly on the food groups and proportions given below.

A BALANCED DIET

The diagram on the right shows the proportions of each type of food a child needs in order to get a healthy balanced diet – approximately one-third grains and potatoes, one-third fruit and vegetables and one-third divided equally between protein- and calcium-rich foods. If your kids eat foods in these proportions, and a wide variety of each type of food, then they should be getting all the essential nutrients they need for good health.

You may be surprised to see a small segment is included for fatty, sugary foods. As long as the majority of your child's diet is made up of nutritious foods, it is okay to include these occasionally. It is important that no food is seen to be 'banned' or 'bad' otherwise your kids will award it forbidden fruit status and want to eat it the most.

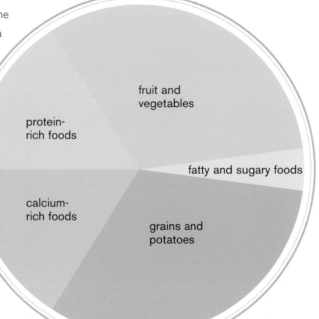

fruit and vegetables

protein-rich foods

fatty and sugary foods

calcium-rich foods

grains and potatoes

GRAINS AND POTATOES

Starchy carbohydrates, such as bread, cereals, rice, pasta, potatoes and pulses, are broken down by the body to form its main source of energy, glucose. Unfortunately, many carbohydrate-rich foods available today have been highly refined, a process which not only strips them of much of their vitamin, mineral and fibre content, but also increases the speed at which they release their sugars into the blood stream. The body is programmed to ensure that blood sugar levels remain relatively stable, so when we eat these fast-releasing sugars the body responds by secreting large amounts of the sugar-lowering hormone, insulin. As a result, the rising blood sugar levels plummet leaving us tired and listless. Children are particularly affected by fluctuating blood sugar levels and often show signs of fidgeting, hyperactivity, shouting or aggression as levels surge, followed by tiredness, temper tantrums and a lack of concentration as they fall.

This yo-yo effect can generally be avoided by replacing refined carbohydrates with unrefined ones, such as stoneground bread, wholegrain cereals and wholewheat pasta. These wholefood alternatives are not only broken down by the body more slowly, resulting in a more sustained release of energy, they are also far richer in fibre, B vitamins (needed for growth and energy), iron, magnesium and immune-boosting zinc.

12 EASY WAYS TO INCREASE FRUIT AND VEGETABLE INTAKE

1 Liquidize vegetables to make soups or pasta sauces (pages 74, 86 and 89)

2 Purée fruits to make compotes (page 121) to be stirred into yoghurt, porridge, custard or ice cream or spooned onto cereals and puddings

3 Make fresh fruit smoothies for breakfast, snacks or pudding (page 42)

4 Make freshly squeezed fruit and vegetable juices (page 68)

5 Chop raw vegetables, such as peppers and celery, into sticks and serve as crudités for dips (page 48)

6 Make your own pizza and top it with a variety of vegetables, such as spinach, courgettes and tomatoes (page 82)

7 Mash together a few boiled root vegetables, such as carrots, sweet potatoes, parsnips and swede and serve this instead of mashed potato

8 Make your own vegetable burgers (page 109)

9 Make vegetable dippers out of root vegetables such as parsnips, sweet potatoes or carrots (page 51)

10 Purée fresh fruits and freeze to make iced lollies (page 139) or use as a substitute for ice cream

11 Add extra vegetables to meals your children like, such as corn kernels and spinach to fish pie

12 Top breakfast cereals, ice cream or yoghurt with slices of fresh fruit

Did You Know?

The brain relies entirely on broken-down carbohydrates (glucose) to function, so when blood sugar levels fall, concentration levels and behaviour are directly affected. This is just one more reason why slower-releasing carbohydrates are essential to your child's diet.

FRUIT AND VEGETABLES

Rich in vitamins and minerals, fruit and vegetables are also great sources of phytochemicals, which help to keep the immune system strong and protect against a whole host of illnesses and diseases. Rather than focusing on any one fruit or vegetable, try to include as many different coloured ones as possible to ensure that your child gets a wide variety of nutrients.

PROTEIN-RICH FOODS

Essential for healthy growth and the development and repair of skin, muscle and other tissues, protein is a vitally important part of a growing child's diet. Foods rich in protein include meat, poultry, fish, dairy products, eggs, nuts, seeds, beans and pulses.

CALCIUM-RICH FOODS

The mineral calcium is important for building strong, healthy bones and teeth. Calcium-rich foods also provide several of the B vitamins as well as vitamin A and D. Good sources of calcium include dairy products, eggs, canned sardines with bones, pulses, nuts, dried fruit, leafy green vegetables, tofu and wholegrains.

The saturated fat content of calcium-rich dairy foods can be reduced for children over the age of five by using semi-skimmed milk and low fat yoghurt and cheese. However, children under five need the full-fat versions because they need the extra calories and vitamins that these provide.

ESSENTIAL FATTY ACIDS

Omega 3 and omega 6 fats, known as essential fatty acids, can't be made in the body so they must be supplied by the diet. They are vital for children's health as they help to boost the immune system, build healthy cells and discourage allergies. Omega 6 fats are found in oils – such as safflower, sesame, sunflower, grapeseed, soya and corn – nuts and seeds.

Omega 3 fats in particular are needed for healthy brain growth and development. In fact, recent research indicates that these fats may be so influential on the development of brain and central nervous tissue that a diet rich in them may result in fewer temper tantrums and an increased ability to concentrate, especially in kids who already have a history of attention deficit disorder and hyperactivity. Omega 3 fats are found in oily fish, such as mackerel, sardines and salmon, leafy green vegetables, sweet potatoes, wholegrains, beans, linseeds, linseed oil, walnuts, walnut oil, rapeseed oil, olives and olive oil.

HOW TO ENSURE KIDS GET ALL THE ESSENTIAL FATTY ACIDS THEY NEED

Give oily fish, such as salmon, herring, sardines or mackerel, to your children once or twice a week. Because oily fish can harbour harmful substances called dioxins, it is recommended that boys under 16 consume no more than four portions of oily fish a week and girls no more than two (this is because dioxin levels can accumulate in the body and may harm an unborn child in the future).

Encourage your children to snack on nuts and seeds and include them in breakfast cereals, cakes and biscuits, and sprinkle them on top of salads.

Spread peanut butter on toast.

Give kids plenty of fresh vegetables, especially leafy green varieties.

Use nut or seed oils in salad dressings.

HOW MUCH DO CHILDREN NEED TO EAT?

This chart is to be used as a guide only – some children will eat slightly
more, some slightly less. Younger children usually need to eat slightly less
than older ones so the exact size of a portion will vary, too.

FOOD GROUP	SERVINGS PER DAY	EXAMPLES OF A SERVING
grains and potatoes	4–6	**one serving is approximately the size of a child's fist, for example:** 1 slice of bread • 1 small bread roll • 3–4 tablespoons cooked pasta or rice • 2–3 tablespoons (25 g) breakfast cereal • a fist-sized potato or sweet potato I 2 crackers
vegetables	3	**one serving is approximately the amount a child can hold in one hand, for example:** 2–3 tablespoons raw or cooked vegetables • about 30 g raw leafy vegetables, such as spinach or lettuce • 1 medium tomato or 3–5 cherry tomatoes • 1 medium glass of vegetable juice (175 ml)
fruit	2	**one serving is approximately the amount a child can hold in one hand, for example:** ½ grapefruit, mango or papaya • 1 medium apple, pear, kiwi, satsuma, peach, banana or plum • 2–3 tablespoons smaller fruits, such as grapes, berries or blackcurrants • 2–3 tablespoons dried fruit • 2–3 tablespoons canned fruit • 1 medium glass of fruit juice (175 ml)
calcium-rich foods	2	**one serving is approximately the size of a child's fist, for example:** 1 medium glass of milk (150 ml) • 1 yoghurt (100 ml) • a piece of cheese or tofu (about 30 g) • 1–2 tablespoons canned sardines
protein-rich foods	2	**one serving is approximately the size of a child's palm, for example:** 1 slice of lean meat (40–80 g) • 2 thin slices of chicken or turkey (40–80 g) • a piece of fish about half the size of a child's palm • 1 large egg • a small handful of nuts or seeds • 1 soya burger or sausage • 2–3 tablespoons soya mince • 2–3 tablespoons pulses

WHAT KIDS SHOULD AVOID?

There are certain things that appear all-too-frequently in many processed foods that do our children more harm than good. Unfortunately, these unwanted elements are often found in even greater quantities in foods that are targeted specifically at our children. Here's what to avoid whenever you can.

TOO MUCH SALT

There is now overwhelming evidence to show that a diet high in salt leads to high blood pressure, stroke and heart disease. It is also linked to an increased risk of osteoporosis and has been shown to aggravate asthma. Despite this, 50 per cent of children are routinely consuming more than twice the recommended level of salt.

Children's high intake of salt is largely due to the amount of processed foods they are eating, most of which has salt added to it by the manufacturer. Also, foods specifically marketed at children, such as canned baked beans and pasta shapes, fish fingers and chicken nuggets, often have an even higher salt content than the adult versions.

AGE	MAXIMUM DAILY SALT INTAKE
up to 12 months	1 g
1–6 years	2 g
7–14 years	less than 5 g

HOW TO CUT BACK

- Given that 75 to 80 per cent of the salt we eat is hidden in processed foods, the most effective way to reduce salt intake is to cut back on these as much as possible and to replace them with fresh, natural alternatives. This is a particularly effective way of reducing the salt intake of kids because they generally eat a large amount of processed foods.
- Replace processed meats, such as salami, sausages and burgers, with unsalted fish, fresh chicken, turkey, lamb and beef.
- Replace processed cheeses, cheesy snacks and feta cheese with cream cheese, natural cottage cheese, Cheddar and mozzarella.
- Replace crisps, salted nuts and other salty snacks with unsalted mixed nuts, dried fruit, unsalted crackers and raw vegetables.
- Replace canned foods, especially baked beans, canned pastas and commercially prepared soups and sauces, with home-made alternatives.

FOOD	SALT PER CHILD SERVING
chicken nuggets	1.75 g
pizza	1.25 g
doughnut	1.2 g
burger	2 g
milkshake	0.5 g
frosted cereal	1.5 g

TOO MUCH SUGAR

Eighty-three per cent of children eat more added sugars than the maximum level recommended for adults. Sugars come in many forms; they may be called sucrose, glucose, maltose, fructose, dextrose, glucose syrup, corn syrup, hydrolysed starch, inverted sugar or concentrated fruit juice. So when checking a food label for sugar, make sure you look for these 'hidden' sugars.

The biggest known health problem caused by too much sugar in children's diets is the appearance of dental caries. However, foods high in sugar are also often high in fat or alternatively low in essential nutrients, therefore they fill a child up with 'empty calories' while leaving less room for other more nutritious foods. As a result, a diet high in sugar is often linked to poor nutritional intake and obesity. Ideally, only 10 per cent of a child's daily calories should come from sugar in any form.

AGE	MAXIMUM DAILY SUGAR INTAKE
4–6 years	40 g (8 teaspoons)
7–10 years	46 g (9 teaspoons)
11+ years	50 g (10 teaspoons)

HOW TO CUT BACK

- Check food labels for hidden sugars, such as sucrose, glucose, maltose, dextrose, lactose, syrup, corn syrup, hydrolysed starch, inverted sugar, fructose or concentrated fruit juice, and choose foods that contain less than 2 g sugar per 100 g.
- Only add sugar to food when necessary. Try sweetening foods in other ways, for example by adding dried fruit to cakes, or mashed bananas to natural yoghurt.
- Home-made puddings are likely to contain much less added sugar than commercially made ones so make your own whenever

possible. Alternatively, offer fresh or dried fruit, or canned fruit in its own juice.
- Replace sugary drinks with water, unsweetened fruit juice diluted with still or sparkling water, fresh fruit smoothies and home-made juices (pages 42 and 68).
- Swap processed, sugary breakfast cereals for lower sugar alternatives, such as whole bran and wholewheat cereals, home-made muesli (page 32) and porridge oats.
- Keep high-sugar snacks like biscuits and fruit bars to a minimum and replace them with home-made or savoury alternatives (pages 60–67) or fresh fruit.

FOOD YOU LEAST EXPECT TO CONTAIN HIGH LEVELS OF SUGAR

FOOD	SUGAR
1 generous helping of commercially prepared tomato ketchup	1 teaspoon
1 child serving of baked beans	2½ teaspoons
1 small pot of flavoured yoghurt	up to 4 teaspoons
1 child serving of vanilla ice cream	3 teaspoons
1 child serving of canned sweetcorn	2 teaspoons

TOO MUCH SATURATED AND HYDROGENATED FAT

Saturated fat – found in meat, meat products, whole milk, hard cheese, butter, lard and cream – raises blood cholesterol levels and increases the risk of heart disease and cancer. Like all fats, at 9 kcal per gram, it is one of the most calorie dense nutrients and therefore increases the likelihood of obesity. Over 90 per cent of children consume more saturated fat than the recommended level for adults.

Hydrogenated fats are vegetable oils that have been artificially hardened during the manufacturing process. Manufacturers like to use them because they are cheap and can increase a food's shelf life. Consequently, they are often found in commercially prepared cakes, biscuits, margarines and puddings. However, this 'new' fat has been shown to be even more harmful to the body than saturated fat because not only does it raise levels of 'bad' cholesterol (as does saturated fat) but it also reduces levels of 'good' cholesterol, therefore doubling the risk of heart disease. Recent food surveys have shown that foods specifically targeted at children are often particularly high in hydrogenated fats.

The amount of saturated and hydrogenated fat in your child's diet should be kept to a minimum. Ideally, these foods should make up no more than 10 per cent of a child's daily calorie intake.

HOW TO CUT BACK

To reduce saturated fat:

- Cut back on cakes, biscuits, crisps, chocolate, ice cream and processed foods, especially processed meats.

To reduce hydrogenated fat:

- Choose margarines and spreads that contain little or no hydrogenated fat (check the label).
- Bake your own cakes and biscuits. Commercially prepared products contain the most hydrogenated fats of any food.
- Cut back on crisps, ready-prepared snacks and chocolate confectionery as much as possible, all of which can contain relatively high levels of hydrogenated fats.
- Avoid fast food because it is usually fried in partially hydrogenated oil.

MECHANICALLY RECOVERED MEAT

Mechanically recovered meat (MRM) is the meat residue that is left on the carcass of an animal after all the prime cuts have been removed. It is pressure-blasted off the bones and forms a reddish slurry. Some food manufacturers use this as a cheap way to bulk up their meat products. It should be avoided because it contains fewer nutrients than prime cuts of meat.

HOW TO CUT BACK

- Manufacturers must declare whether their products contain MRM, so always read the food label carefully.

CHEAP FILLERS

Manufacturers often keep costs low by bulking out food with cheap fillers, such as maltodextrin, modified starch, starch and modified cornflour, all of which have very little nutritional value. They just serve to fill up small tummies with 'empty calories', leaving less room for more nutritious food.

HOW TO CUT BACK

- By cutting back on processed foods, such as cakes, biscuits, crisps and other sugary and savoury snacks, you will automatically cut back on cheap fillers such as these.

ADDITIVES

On average, we eat about 3.6 kg of food additives per person every year. The negative health effects of children consuming large amounts of additives has not been adequately researched. However, according to a recent government study, some food additives could be responsible for tantrums, excessive fiddling, lack of concentration, interrupting, hyperactivity and difficulty sleeping in up to 25 per cent of all young children. If you feel there could be a connection between your children's behaviour and their diet, exclude foods containing the suspect additives for a couple of weeks and see if you notice an improvement in behaviour.

COLOURINGS

Most artificial colourings are synthetic chemicals that don't occur in nature. The use of colouring usually indicates that no fruit or other natural ingredient has been used. As a result they appear most commonly in foods of low nutritional value, such as sweets, fizzy drinks, jelly and desserts.

Colourings can also cause hyperactivity in some sensitive children. According to a recent government study, the artificial food colourings tartrazine (E102), Sunset Yellow (E110), Carmoisine (E122) and Ponceau 4R (E124) and the preservative sodium benzoate (E211) could be responsible for behavioural changes in children. These controversial red and yellow dyes are likely to be used in products such as birthday cakes with brightly coloured icings. However, many seemingly uncoloured, harmless foods, such as elderflower cordial or canned fruit, may also contain these behaviour-disrupting additives. Always check the food label and try to avoid them wherever possible.

FLAVOURINGS, FLAVOUR ENHANCERS AND ARTIFICIAL SWEETENERS

The word 'flavourings' can be used to describe more than 4,000 chemicals. Many are deemed to be safe although a few can lead to intolerance in some children resulting in asthma, headaches, rashes and eczema. Flavourings are most commonly used in products that are lacking in the real thing. Consequently, like colourings, they often appear in foods of poor nutritional value. Manufacturers often keep the identity of artificial (and natural) flavourings a secret, which can make it difficult to know exactly what you are feeding your children.

Artificial sweeteners are routinely used by manufacturers to flavour foods and drinks because they are even cheaper than sugar. They are less harmful to children's teeth, but they still condition their taste buds into liking intensely sweet foods. Officially, they are deemed to be safe, however tests linking high intakes with increased incidences of cancer and neurological problems has left a question mark hanging over just how safe they are.

PRESERVATIVES

Manufacturers use preservatives to extend the shelf life of foods. There are some natural preservatives available, such as natural acids and salts, but most of the commonly used preservatives are manufactured. The safety of their use in children's foods has not yet been proven, therefore they are best avoided wherever possible. It is known that certain preservatives, such as sulphur dioxide which is often used to stop discolouration in dried fruit, also destroy vitamin B1 and can cause adverse reactions, such as asthma attacks in susceptible children.

HOW TO CUT BACK

- The easiest and most effective way to reduce the number of additives your child consumes is to cut back on the amount of pre-prepared and processed foods they eat and replace them with fresh, natural, home-made alternatives. Only then will you know exactly what your child is consuming. Always read food labels carefully.

PESTICIDES

Exposure to pesticide residues in early life has been linked to a greater risk in later life of cancer, neurological impairment and dysfunction of the immune, endocrine and nervous systems. Children are more vulnerable to pesticide residues in food and drink because not only are their systems immature and in the process of developing, but weight for weight children consume far more of certain foods than adults. This is particularly true for a weaning baby who, weight for weight, will eat considerably more fruit and vegetables than an adult.

Consequently, the exposure of children and babies to pesticide residues is substantially underestimated. This was confirmed in 1998 when the US Environmental Working Group reported that one in every 20 children consumes unsafe levels of organophosphate chemicals every day. A child also has a one-in-four chance of eating a peach with an unsafe dose of pesticides, a one-in-seven chance of eating an apple and a one-in-eight chance of eating a nectarine with an unsafe dose. Many fruit and vegetables contain pesticide residues, but they are also found in products such as breakfast cereals, cereal bars and crisps.

HOW TO CUT BACK

- Choose organic varieties of fruit and vegetables wherever possible (page 19). If possible, why not grow some of your own? You'll be amazed how readily a child will eat something he has grown himself.

ORGANIC FOODS

Children deserve the best possible food made from the safest, healthiest ingredients. Not only are their cells multiplying at their peak as their little bodies grow and their vital organs develop, but a child's kidneys are immature and therefore less able to filter out and break down harmful substances. In addition to this, their nervous systems are rapidly developing, a process that can be disrupted by exposure to toxins. Finally, weight for weight, children consume far higher proportions of many foods than adults.

It is for all these reasons that I recommend buying organic produce wherever availability and finances will allow, especially fruit, vegetables, meat and dairy items. Organic foods are grown without the use of pesticides and chemicals. Animals reared organically will not have been routinely given hormones and antibiotics, so residues from these chemicals will not be found in their meat. You can also be assured that organic foods won't contain genetically modified ingredients, flavourings or colourings. Finally, organic food production is kinder to animals and the environment, therefore when we buy organic, we are helping to ensure that our children inherit a healthier world.

THE SOLUTION

In a world where the food industry spends millions of pounds each year promoting over-processed, fatty, sugary and additive-laden foods to our kids, it is easy as a parent to feel powerless to change what our kids eat. The truth is no one has more influence over your child's eating habits than you, so here is how you can really make a difference.

PREPARE MORE FOOD AT HOME

The single, most effective thing you can do to improve your child's diet is to cut back on pre-prepared and processed foods and make more of it yourself at home from fresh ingredients. This may sound very time consuming but I, as a busy working mother of two, can assure you that it isn't if you follow these three simple steps:

1 Invest in some inexpensive, but essential kitchen items: plastic containers of various sizes that are freezer-, microwave- and dishwasher-proof; airtight tins or jars for storing cakes, biscuits and bread; freezer bags of various sizes; sticky white labels for labelling frozen food.

2 Get into the habit of cooking in bulk and freezing or storing foods for future use. This book is full of fast and healthy recipes made from everyday ingredients that are ideal for cooking in large quantities and freezing.

3 Establish a repertoire of four or five different healthy breakfasts, lunches, evening meals, puddings and snacks that can be whipped up in minutes. Refer to the Real Alternatives lists at the beginning of each recipe chapter for lots of super-speedy ideas for every meal and snack of the day.

CHANGE THE WAY YOU THINK ABOUT FEEDING YOUR CHILDREN

Contrary to popular belief, children are not mini aliens beamed down from another planet that need feeding a special kid-friendly diet of chips, burgers, fish fingers and ice cream. They don't need to be bribed and enticed into eating by brightly coloured packaging, novelty toys or gimmicks. They are mini adults and, like adults, if allowed to experience a wide variety of tastes they will eventually develop a liking for a whole range of different foods.

This applies to babies, too. Therefore it is important to educate our children's taste buds as early as possible by feeding weaning babies on a wide variety of home-cooked foods. Shop-bought jars may have their place occasionally, but if relied upon for every meal they will only encourage your children to develop a bland and unadventurous palette, making the future task of encouraging them to eat a varied diet of real, unprocessed foods that much harder.

Try not to insist that your children eat everything on their plate. Encourage them to start with small amounts and explain that they can always have more if they want it. Research shows that children who are taught to finish everything on their plates often lose the skill to judge for themselves when they are full and consequently can go on to become over-eaters as adults. Instead, if they insist they are full, simply remove the food but do not offer a pudding. Don't assume they won't like a food until they have tried it (unless it is extremely spicy).

SPRING CLEAN YOUR KITCHEN CUPBOARDS

Don't keep unhealthy foods in the house. No matter how good your intentions, if your cupboards, fridge and freezer are filled with food and drinks that are high in fat, salt, sugar and/or additives, they will get eaten. So clear them out and cross them off your future shopping list. Instead, take a look at Storecupboard Basics on pages 26–7, which contains a list of everything you will need to make most of the recipes in this book and doubles as a useful shopping list.

MAKE MEALTIMES FUN

Children enjoy eating with others much more than eating alone, so try to eat with your children whenever you can. Sometimes the very act of sitting at the table together is all that is needed to encourage a child to eat more of the food on his plate.

Eating together also provides an excellent opportunity to encourage children to try new foods and to chat to them about the health benefits of the foods they are eating. Try to talk in terms that are directly relevant to them depending on their age and interests. For example, a younger child may be encouraged by the idea that certain foods will make her grow taller, run faster or jump higher. Older children are often swayed a little more by the way a food may affect their appearance, for example the protein in home-made burgers helping muscles to grow bigger or the vitamins

WAYS TO MAKE MEALTIMES A MORE POSITIVE EXPERIENCE

Involve your children in the social aspect of sharing a meal and talk about subjects you know they are interested in.

Play some music.

Praise, praise, praise. Acknowledge any efforts to try a new food or to eat the foods that are served.

Put a disposal tablecloth on the table and let your kids draw on it with crayons.

in fresh fruit and vegetables helping to make their skin clearer and their eyes brighter.

Children also love to serve themselves. Initially, they may need a little guidance as to quantities but it is amazing how the simple act of being allowed to put their own foods on their plates will entice them to eat.

LEAD BY EXAMPLE

Children learn far more from what they see and experience than from what they are told. Therefore it is vital that parents lead by example when it comes to eating and exercising.

DON'T TAKE REFUSALS TOO SERIOUSLY

Continue to present your children with a wide range of foods even if they resist them at first. If a child refuses to eat a certain food, try not to make too much of an issue of it. Simply take it away and present it again another time, possibly in a different form. For example, a child that doesn't like fresh tomatoes will often happily eat tomato soup.

ENCOURAGE A HEALTHY APPETITE

Most parents worry about their children not eating enough. However, the worst thing you can do is to offer them biscuits, crisps, sweets and fatty, over-processed foods in an attempt to cajole them into eating. Instead, allow them a little time to build up a healthy hunger. After all, a child that comes to the table feeling hungry is far more likely to eat a healthy balanced meal than a child that has been allowed to fill up between meals on junk. Limit snacks to a maximum of two a day (one in the morning between breakfast and lunch and one in the afternoon between lunch and dinner) and make sure the foods available to snack on are as healthy as possible.

Children have only very small stomachs and yet they have huge nutritional needs, so everything they eat should be able to justify its place. Don't have biscuits, chocolate, sweets, sugary drinks and crisps in the house. Instead, make sure the fruit bowl is always topped up and encourage your children to snack on wholemeal toast, natural yoghurt and wholegrain breakfast cereals (more healthy snack ideas can be found on page 45).

Encourage as much physical activity as possible. Children love to move and be active. Unfortunately, the opportunities for them to do so are becoming increasingly limited. Playing outside has been replaced by watching television and time spent playing computer games is increasing. Make time in your family's daily routine for exercise, whether it's walking the dog, a family bike ride or going to the park.

LEGITIMIZE ALL FOODS

Instead of talking to your children about foods being 'good' or 'bad', explain to them that all foods are okay if eaten in the right amounts. If we teach this message to our children, we are a long way towards instilling in them healthy eating habits for life.

COOK TOGETHER

Encourage your children to help you cook. There may be a little more mess in the kitchen than usual, but it's a great way of teaching kids about food. Even very young children will enjoy squidging pizza dough through their fingers or cutting biscuits. You'll be amazed at how much more they'll eat when they've rolled it, shaped it or baked it themselves. By the time a child is four, he should be able to make a simple meal with a bit of help from you, and the skills he learns will stay with him for the rest of his life.

UNDERSTANDING FOOD LABELS

Unfortunately, a lack of current legislation about what has to appear on food labels means that we cannot rely on either the government or the food industry to ensure that the food eaten by our children is nutritious or even safe, so it is essential that we are able to make our own informed decisions. Poor labelling and marketing hype can make it almost impossible for a parent to decipher whether a product is actually healthy or not. The table below is an easy-to-use, handy guide to whether a food contains unhealthy

amounts of fat, sugar and salt. If you are looking at a food that your child is likely to eat in its entirety, like a ready meal, compare the figure per serving given on the package with the guide. For other foods, such as snacks or foods eaten in relatively small amounts, look at the nutritional information per 100 g.

UNDERSTANDING FOOD LABELS		
NUTRIENT	A LOT	A LITTLE
Total fat	20 g	3 g
Saturated fat	5 g	1 g
Sugar	10 g	3 g
Sodium	0.5 g	0.1 g
Salt	1.25 g	0.25 g

KEEP A CAREFUL EYE ON TELEVISION VIEWING

On average, children spend more time in front of the television than being taught at school. The number of food advertisements are two to three times higher during children's programmes than during adult viewing periods and a recent survey of these adverts found that between 95 and 99 per cent of all products advertised are high in fat and/or salt and/or sugar. Additional studies have also found that children who are regularly exposed to these adverts are far less able to judge the nutritional quality of foods. For these reasons, it is important to carefully monitor the amount of television your children watch.

FOOD WARNINGS

Nuts In a small number of children, nuts, especially peanuts, can cause serious allergies. Children under the age of three with a family history of allergy should not be given peanuts in any form. Children with no allergy history can be given peanuts and other nuts after the age of one. Don't give whole nuts to any child under the age of five because of the risk of choking. Always chop nuts or grind them finely.

Eggs Don't give raw eggs or food that contains raw or partially cooked eggs to young children because of the risk of salmonella, which causes food poisoning. If you give eggs to your toddler, make sure they are hard boiled so both the white and yolk are solid.

Honey Don't give honey to children under the age of one. Occasionally, honey can contain a type of bacteria that can produce toxins in a baby's intestines causing serious illness.

YOUR KITCHEN

It can be frustrating to open a recipe book and find that your cupboards only contain half the ingredients and equipment called for. That's why I have included a list of all the things you will need to make the recipes in this book. The list may seem long, but it contains lots of useful, basic items that every kitchen should have. I also hope that the information in this book about many of the commercially prepared foods you may currently have in your freezer and cupboards is enough to convince you that they can go, making room for these healthier foods.

STORECUPBOARD BASICS

RICE, GRAINS & CEREALS
Brown rice
Basmati rice
Bulghur wheat
Rolled oats
Wheat bran
High bran cereals
One hundred per cent
    whole-wheat cereals

BEANS & PULSES
Any canned or dried beans,
    including red kidney,
    butter, cannellini, haricot,
    aduki, borlotti, pinto,
    and chickpeas
Red and green split lentils

BREAD
Wholemeal bread
Flour tortillas
Wholemeal pita bread
Linseed rye bread
Wholemeal fruit buns

PASTA & NOODLES
Whole-wheat pasta – different
    shapes and sizes such as
    penne, spaghetti, farfalle
Couscous
Noodles (any sort)

NUTS & SEEDS
Brazil nuts
Cashew nuts

Flaked almonds
Hazelnuts
Mixed nuts
Pecan nuts
Unsalted peanuts
Walnuts
Linseed
Poppy seeds
Pumpkin seeds
Sesame seeds
Sunflower seeds

DAIRY & EGGS
Eggs
Milk
Half fat crème fraîche
Fromage frais

Natural yoghurt
Cottage cheese
Low fat Cheddar cheese
Soft cheeses

MEAT, POULTRY & FISH
Parma ham and bacon
Lean minced beef
Extra lean ham and turkey
    slices (fresh from the deli
    counter, not processed)
Chicken breast (skin removed)
Mackerel and sardines (canned
    and fresh)
Smoked salmon
Wild or organic salmon
    fillets

Tuna (canned in spring water
and fresh)
Cod (frozen or fresh)
Haddock (frozen or fresh)

FRUIT

Any, particularly apples, pears,
plums, cherries, peaches,
strawberries, raspberries,
blackberries, kiwi fruit,
oranges, limes, lemons,
grapefruit, red grapes
Canned fruit in fruit juice rather
than syrup
Frozen mixed berries
Dried fruit, including ready-to-
eat apricots, dates, figs,
raisins and sultanas

VEGETABLES

As many different coloured
fresh vegetables as possible
Potatoes and sweet potatoes
Frozen vegetables – these can
be just as nutritious as fresh
ones and meals can be made
from them in no time

HERBS & FLAVOURINGS

A choice of fresh herbs, such as
coriander, mint, basil, parsley
Garlic
Ginger
Mild curry powder
Ground cumin

BAKING

Wholemeal flour
Strong white bread flour

Oatmeal
Baking powder
Mixed spice
Ground ginger
Ground cinnamon

FATS & OILS

Virgin olive oil, for cooking
Sunflower oil, for cooking
and baking
Extra virgin cold pressed olive
oil for use in salad dressings
Polyunsaturated spread or
sunflower margarine
Unsalted butter

STAPLES

Vegetable stock cubes
Soy sauce
Worcestershire sauce
Tomato purée
Olives
Balsamic vinegar
Red wine vinegar
Good quality plain chocolate
with 70 per cent cocoa solids
Peanut butter (wholefood
varieties are lower in salt
and saturated fat than regular
peanut butter)
Honey
Canned tomatoes
Cornflour

DRINKS

Unsweetened fresh fruit and
vegetable juices, preferably
with pulp
Sparkling mineral water

ESSENTIAL EQUIPMENT

You will probably have most of this equipment in your kitchen
already. When it comes to essential items, buy the best you
can afford so that they will last.

Freezer
Freezerproof and
microwaveable plastic
food containers in
various sizes
Cling film, baking parchment
and aluminium foil
Plastic food bags
Sticky labels
Food processor
Blender
Weighing scales –
electronic scales are ideal
because they are easy for
children to use
Lightweight plastic or
metal bowls
Measuring jug
Set of American cup
measures (these are
useful for children who
are too young to use
weighing scales)
Rolling pin
Assorted biscuit cutters
Steamer
Non-stick frying pan

Non-stick wok with lid
3 saucepans – small,
medium and large
Stove-top grill pan
2 baking sheets
Non-stick roasting tin
Assorted cake and
bread tins
Wire cooling rack
Paper cake cases
Large chopping board
Set of sharp knives
Garlic crusher
Can opener
Potato masher
Box grater
Colander
Sieve
2 wooden spoons
2 tablespoons
2 teaspoons
Slotted metal spoon
Plastic spatula
A solid chair or stool for
your child to stand on to
reach work surface height
6 ramekins – 150 ml

OPTIONAL EQUIPMENT

Microwave
Yoghurt maker
Ice cream maker
Bread maker

Mortar and pestle
Mini blender for making
pesto and grinding nuts
and seeds

RECIPES

BREAKFAST

A GOOD START TO THE DAY

Breakfast is arguably the most important meal of the day, especially for children. Even when we are asleep our bodies continue to burn calories. Children generally sleep for long periods, so by the time they wake up their blood sugar levels are naturally depleted. As breakfast provides a major part of a child's daily energy supply, if breakfast is skipped it can result in lethargy, mood swings, food cravings, excessive hunger and an impaired ability to think and learn. Research shows that kids who eat breakfast are less inclined to crave fatty, sugary foods and are more likely to meet their daily requirements of certain essential vitamins and minerals than those who skip it.

GETTING IT RIGHT

The nutritional quality of commercially prepared breakfast cereals varies wildly from one packet to the next. Some offer a highly nutritious, vitamin-, mineral- and fibre-packed start to your child's day, while the majority are little more than highly processed junk full of fat, sugar and salt. A recent survey of 28 breakfast cereals marketed specifically at children found nearly one-third of them contained 40 per cent sugar and 64 per cent had excessive amounts of salt.

Many of the sugary, processed cereals targeted at children have been so highly refined that they are not only stripped of most of their natural goodness, they are also broken down by the body very quickly when eaten. This causes blood sugar levels to surge and then plummet, which in turn can result in behavioural problems and hyperactivity followed by tiredness, tantrums and an inability to concentrate.

The best way to avoid this roller coaster effect on blood sugar levels is to encourage kids to eat foods that release their sugars more slowly into the blood stream, such as wholewheat cereals, oats, fruit and wholemeal bread. Breakfast consisting of these foods will ensure your child has a steady supply of energy to draw on throughout the morning.

CEREALS
REAL ALTERNATIVES
bran flakes soaked in milk, served with yoghurt and fresh raspberries • 100 per cent wholegrain shredded wheat biscuits with chopped dried apricots • porridge • wholewheat biscuits with warm milk, sliced banana and sultanas

EGGS AND TOAST
REAL ALTERNATIVES
boiled eggs mashed with some chopped organic ham spread on wholemeal toast • wholemeal hot cross bun, toasted and lightly buttered • toasted wholemeal muffin spread with tahini paste and honey

FRUIT AND YOGHURT
REAL ALTERNATIVES
Greek or natural yoghurt flavoured with fruit compote, fresh fruit, dried apricots, honey or finely chopped nuts and seeds • hot fruit kebabs with honey, a sprinkling of sesame seeds and Greek yoghurt • a halved kiwi fruit served in 2 egg cups with a teaspoon and some wholemeal toast • warm fruit compote (page 121), blended with a banana and a dollop of half fat crème fraîche • 1 chopped apple and 1 pear mixed with sultanas, heated in a microwave until soft, then mixed with Greek yoghurt and cinnamon

AVOID	REPLACE WITH
Cereals marketed specifically at kids, especially those described as 'frosted', and chocolate cereals	Products labelled 'wholewheat' or 'whole bran', porridge oats or home-made Muesli (page 32)
Commercially prepared breakfast bars	Home-made alternatives (page 32)
White bread	Wholemeal, nutty or stoneground varieties
Sweetened yoghurts and those marketed specifically at kids	Natural or Greek yoghurt or fromage frais flavoured with honey, natural fruit purée or fresh fruit
Flavoured milks and commercial milkshakes	Plain milk, home-made smoothies and milkshakes

BREAKFAST BARS

These bars make a great snack at any time of the day or include them in packed lunches.

PREPARATION TIME 12–15 minutes
COOKING TIME 15–20 minutes

175 g porridge oats

50 g sultanas

75 g ready-to-eat dried apricots, finely chopped

50 g dried papaya, finely chopped

50 g pitted dates, finely chopped

25 g flaked almonds

25 g sesame seeds

2 tablespoons clear honey

3 tablespoons smooth peanut butter

1 egg white

a baking tin, 25 × 20 cm, lightly greased and base-lined with non-stick baking parchment

makes 14 bars

Put the oats in a large bowl. Add all the dried fruit, nuts and seeds and mix well.

Put the honey and peanut butter in a small saucepan and heat gently, stirring occasionally with a wooden spoon until smooth. Pour into the oat mixture and mix well.

Put the egg white in a small bowl and beat with a wire whisk until light and frothy. Add it to the oat mixture and mix with a wooden spoon until the mixture sticks together. Spoon the mixture into the prepared tin, then press it down with the back of the spoon, making the surface as even as possible.

Bake in a preheated oven at 190°C (375°F) Gas 5 for 15–20 minutes until the top is golden and feels firm to the touch. Remove from the oven and let cool slightly in the tin before cutting into 14 bars. Let cool completely before removing them from the tin. Store the bars in an airtight container for up to 5 days.

MUESLI

Breakfasts don't come more nutrient-packed than this. The nuts and seeds are full of vitamins, minerals and essential fatty acids. The oats and wheatgerm will stabilize blood sugars and provide a constant source of energy throughout the morning and the dried fruit is a fabulous source of fibre helping to keep all the digestive processes working properly. Add to that the calcium-rich milk or yoghurt and sliced fresh fruit – you couldn't give your family a better start to the day.

PREPARATION TIME 10 minutes
COOKING TIME 10–15 minutes

50 g sunflower seeds

50 g pumpkin seeds

25 g linseed

50 g flaked almonds

50 g hazelnuts, chopped

450 g porridge oats

50 g wheatgerm

75 g ready-to-eat dried apricots, chopped

50 g dried banana

50 g golden sultanas

50 g dried cherries or cranberries

to serve

1 banana, sliced, or a small handful of fresh berries or seedless grapes

cold milk or natural yoghurt

2 baking sheets

makes 950 g

Sprinkle all the seeds and nuts on one baking sheet and the oats on another. Cook in a preheated oven at 200°C (400°F) Gas 6 for 10–15 minutes or until lightly toasted. Remove from the oven and let cool.

Once cool, put the nuts, seeds and oats in a large airtight container. Add the wheatgerm and all the dried fruit, then either stir to mix or close the lid securely and shake well. Store in a cool dry cupboard until required.

To serve, spoon about 5 tablespoons muesli into a cereal bowl, top with fresh fruit and pour over some milk or add some natural yoghurt.

COOK'S TIP

- This is a recipe which children can help to make. Don't worry about being too exact with the measurements. Use American measuring cups to make the ingredients easier to measure. You will need approximately 3 cups oats and 1/3 cup each of the nuts and 1/4 cup each of the dried fruit.

VARIATIONS

- This can also be served as a dry snack, without the milk or yoghurt, in small paper bags instead of salted peanuts or crisps.
- Use as a topping to add crunch to yoghurts.
- **Granola** Put all the muesli ingredients in a large bowl and add 2 tablespoons maple syrup. Mix well. Transfer to a non-stick baking sheet and bake in a preheated oven at 160°C (325°F) Gas 3 for about 40 minutes, stirring halfway through, until crisp and golden. Serve with cold milk.

PINK PORRIDGE

Oats are an excellent source of slow-releasing sugars as well as fibre, iron, zinc and B vitamins. By adding some fresh fruit, you are making an already excellent breakfast even more nutritious and adding novelty value at the same time!

PREPARATION TIME 5 minutes
COOKING TIME 4–5 minutes, plus 2 minutes standing time

75 g porridge oats

25 g wheat bran

600 ml milk (see cook's tips)

75 g strawberries, hulled, or raspberries, plus extra for serving

1–2 teaspoons clear honey (optional)

serves 2–4

Put the oats, bran and milk in a large microwaveable bowl and cover with microwaveable wrap. Pierce the wrap and heat in a microwave on HIGH for 4–5 minutes. Stir and let stand for 2 minutes.

Transfer the porridge to a blender, add the fruit and process until smooth. Add honey, if using, to taste. If necessary, return the porridge to the microwaveable bowl and reheat on HIGH for 1 minute.

To serve, spoon into individual bowls and top with a few whole strawberries or raspberries.

COOK'S TIPS
- Use whole milk for children under the age of 5, semi-skimmed milk for children over 5.
- To make the porridge on the hob, pour the milk into a non-stick saucepan and sprinkle in the oats and wheat bran. Heat gently, stirring occasionally, for 2–3 minutes until thickened. Let cool slightly, then add the fruit and honey. Transfer to a blender and process until smooth.

VARIATION
- Replace the strawberries or raspberries with 1 sliced banana and ½ teaspoon ground cinnamon.

OVERNIGHT OATS

This is very simple to make. It can be whipped up in minutes and provides an excellent alternative to many of the sugar- and salt-laden commercially prepared breakfast cereals.

PREPARATION TIME 10 minutes
COOKING TIME 3–4 minutes

base mixture

225 g porridge oats

50 g wheat bran

50 g linseed

50 g sunflower seeds

50 g golden sultanas

25 g finely chopped mixed nuts

to serve, per 50 g serving
300 ml semi-skimmed milk (use whole milk for children under 5)

½ apple, peeled, cored and grated

1 tablespoon natural yoghurt

fresh fruit, such as apricots and berries

makes 475 g; serves 8

Put all the ingredients for the base mixture in an airtight container and close securely. Shake well to mix, then store in a cool cupboard until required.

The night before you want to serve the oats, put 3 tablespoons of the mixture in a bowl and cover with 150 ml milk. Stir in the grated apple, cover the bowl with plastic wrap and leave in the refrigerator overnight.

The following morning, add a little more milk to the bowl to slacken the mixture. Transfer the mixture to a non-stick saucepan and heat gently, stirring, until hot, 3–4 minutes. Alternatively, put the mixture in a microwaveable bowl and heat in a microwave on HIGH for 2 minutes. Stir, then let stand for 1 minute.

To serve, top with the yoghurt and some fresh fruit.

COOK'S TIP
- If you prefer a nutty, crisp texture, omit the nuts from the base mix and sprinkle them on top, to serve.

APPLE & OAT MUFFINS

These muffins are made with sunflower oil and yoghurt, so they are moist without having the high saturated fat content of most commercially prepared versions. Serve them warm on a cold morning or eat them as a snack at any time of the day. They also make a delicious pudding, served with some Home-made Custard (page 126) or warm fruit compote (page 121) and a dollop of half fat crème fraîche.

PREPARATION TIME 5 minutes
COOKING TIME 15–18 minutes

100 g wholemeal self-raising flour

100 g white self-raising flour

2 teaspoons baking powder

1 teaspoon mixed spice

25 g wheat bran

50 g light muscovado sugar

50 g sultanas

2 apples, about 225 g, cored and finely chopped

25 g pecan nuts, chopped

50 g pitted dates, chopped

120 ml sunflower oil

2 eggs, beaten

2 tablespoons natural yoghurt

1 tablespoon sesame seeds

a 12-hole muffin tin, lined with 12 paper muffin cases

makes 12

Sift the flours, baking powder and mixed spice into a large bowl. Add any bran left in the sieve and the wheat bran and mix.

Add the sugar, sultanas, apples, pecans and dates and mix lightly with a wooden spoon. Make a well in the centre, add the oil and eggs and stir to mix. Add the yoghurt and stir lightly, until just mixed (do not overmix or the muffins will be dry).

Spoon the mixture into the paper cases until three-quarters full. Sprinkle the sesame seeds over the top, then bake in a preheated oven at 200°C (400°F) Gas 6 for 15–18 minutes until firm to the touch. Remove from the oven and let cool slightly. Serve warm. The muffins can be wrapped and frozen for up to 1 month.

COOK'S TIP
- Bake ahead of time, then reheat in a microwave on HIGH for 20–25 seconds.

VARIATIONS
- Replace the apples with 2 ripe mashed bananas and use extra chopped dates instead of the sultanas.
- Replace the sultanas with chopped dried fruit, such as apricots, papaya or mango and use coconut flakes in place of the pecans. Sprinkle flaked almonds over the top before baking.
- Use ground ginger, ground cinnamon or finely grated orange or lemon zest in place of the mixed spice.

Did You Know?

Apples and oats are two excellent foods to eat for breakfast because they both have a very low rating on the glycaemic index. This means that after being eaten they release their sugars very slowly into the blood stream, which helps to keep energy levels constant all morning and hunger pangs at bay.

EASY PEASY WHOLEMEAL BREAD

Many of the breads available today have been so highly refined that even the wholemeal varieties release their sugars far too quickly into the blood stream. Many also contain preservatives to increase their shelf life, salt to add taste and colourings to make them look more appealing. Home-made bread on the other hand is free from all those unnecessary additives, is great fun to make and not as difficult as you might think.

PREPARATION TIME
25 minutes, plus 1 hour
proving time
COOKING TIME 40–45 minutes

900 g stoneground wholemeal
bread flour

450 g strong white bread flour,
plus extra for sprinkling
and dusting

2 sachets (6 teaspoons) quick
acting yeast

1 tablespoon sea salt

2 tablespoons light
muscovado sugar

100 g linseed

6 tablespoons olive oil

900 ml warm water

1 tablespoon poppy, sesame or
sunflower seeds

*2 large baking sheets, greased,
or 2 loaf tins, 900 g each,
greased*

makes 2 large loaves

Sift the flours into a large bowl, adding the bran left in the sieve. Stir in the yeast, salt, sugar and linseed. Make a well in the flour and pour in the olive oil and the warm water. Gradually mix the flour into the liquid with your hands until the mixture comes together to make a ball.

Turn the dough out onto a lightly floured work surface and knead thoroughly for 10 minutes until the dough feels smooth and very elastic. Divide the dough in half. Gently shape the dough into 2 neat balls and set the loaves on the prepared baking sheets. Alternatively, they can be shaped into 2 cylinders and put in the loaf tins. Put the sheets or tins in large, lightly oiled plastic bags and leave in a warm place out of any draughts for at least 1 hour or until the loaves have doubled in size.

Uncover the loaves, brush the tops with a little water and sprinkle with the seeds of your choice. Bake in a preheated oven at 230°C (450°F) Gas 8 for 15 minutes, then reduce the heat to 200°C (400°F) Gas 6 and bake for a further 25–30 minutes until golden brown. To test if the loaves are cooked, turn them upside down and tap your knuckles on the base of the loaf. It should sound hollow.

Remove the loaves from the oven, transfer to a wire rack and let cool completely before cutting. Home-made bread is best eaten on the day it's made. Once completely cold, wrap the loaves and store them in an earthenware or wooden bread box.

COOK'S TIPS
- For crusty loaves, leave them to cool uncovered; for a soft crust, cover with a dry tea towel, then let cool.
- The loaves can be frozen for up to 1 month. Let thaw thoroughly and warm through, if liked, before serving.

VARIATIONS
- Add 50 g sunflower seeds and 25 g sesame seeds to the basic bread mix.
- Add 100 g chopped walnuts and 100 g finely chopped pitted dates to the basic bread mix.
- Add 225 g finely chopped mixed dried fruit, such as sultanas, apricots and raisins to the basic bread mix.
- Add 4 tablespoons freshly chopped herbs to the basic bread mix. Try rosemary, parsley and thyme, or sage, thyme and chives, or use a herb-flavoured olive oil.
- Instead of the olive oil, use walnut oil and add 225 g finely chopped walnuts to the basic bread mix.
- For a richer loaf, replace some of the wholemeal flour with spelt, add a beaten egg to the basic bread mix and use milk instead of the water.
- Shape the dough into small round rolls and bake for 10–15 minutes.
- Make bread sticks to use as dippers (page 48).

Did You Know?
Wholemeal flour has twice as much potassium, nearly three times more fibre and six times more magnesium than white flour.

EGGS

Eggs are nature's 'fast food'. One egg can provide up to 20 per cent of a child's daily protein requirement. They also contain potassium, iodine, folic acid, beta-carotene and iron. They can be whipped up in minutes to provide many different nutritious meals. Buy organic eggs whenever possible because not only are they naturally richer in omega 3 fatty acids, they come from chickens that have been fed on a natural diet, free from the large amounts of growth-promoting antibiotics routinely fed to non-organic chickens.

DIPPY EGGS

To prevent eggs from cracking when put in boiling water, make sure they are at room temperature before cooking.

Put an egg on a tablespoon and carefully lower into a saucepan three-quarters full of gently simmering water. For soft boiled eggs, cook for 4 minutes. Remove the egg from the water with a large tablespoon, place it in an egg cup and tap firmly on the shell to crack it and stop the egg from cooking further.

If you prefer hard boiled eggs, cook for 10 minutes in boiling water.

Serve with fingers of wholemeal toast.

COOK'S TIP
• Don't give soft boiled eggs to young children. Make sure both the white and yolk are solid.

PREPARATION TIME 5 minutes
COOKING TIME 8 minutes

2 eggs

1 tablespoon water or milk

2 teaspoons virgin olive oil

50 g lean ham, chopped

sea salt and freshly ground black pepper

an omelette pan or small frying pan, 15 cm diameter

serves 1–2

HAM OMELETTE

Break the eggs into a bowl, add the water or milk and salt and pepper to taste. Whisk briefly with a fork or a wire whisk.

Heat the oil in the omelette or frying pan and swirl it around to coat the bottom of the pan. Pour in the egg mixture, then use a fork to pull the set egg mixture that forms at the edges of the pan into the centre, letting the uncooked egg flow back to the edges. When lightly set, sprinkle in the ham and cook for a further 2 minutes. Fold the omelette over and slide it onto a warmed plate. Serve immediately.

VARIATIONS
• Add 1 chopped tomato with the ham.
• Add 2 tablespoons grated half fat Cheddar cheese when you add the ham.
• Add 1 tablespoon chopped fresh mixed herbs to the eggs before pouring them into the pan.

POACHED EGGS

Half fill a frying pan with water and bring to the boil. Reduce to a gentle simmer, then add a little lemon juice or vinegar to the water. Break an egg into a cup then pour it carefully into the pan.

Alternatively, put some lightly greased round pastry cutters in the water and slip the eggs into these. Cook for 4–5 minutes or until cooked to your liking. Remove with a slotted spoon and serve.

SCRAMBLED EGGS

Beat 1 egg with 1 tablespoon milk and a little black pepper, to taste. Melt a small knob of polyunsaturated spread in a small saucepan or heat 1 teaspoon virgin olive oil until hot. Pour in the beaten egg and cook, stirring continuously, for 2–3 minutes until set and creamy.

Alternatively, put the egg mixture in a microwaveable bowl and heat in a microwave on HIGH for 2 minutes, stirring halfway through.

Serve on top of wholemeal toast.

SMOOTHIES

Smoothies can be a great way of encouraging otherwise reluctant children to eat breakfast. They are also a fabulous way of increasing the amount of fruit your child eats. Here are a few ideas to start you off, but let your children experiment with a whole range of fruit and other ingredients until they find one that they really like.

SUMMER BERRY BREAKFAST

PREPARATION TIME 5 minutes

100 g fresh berries, such as strawberries or raspberries

150 g natural yoghurt

300 ml semi-skimmed milk, chilled (use whole milk for children under 5)

2 tablespoons crushed ice, to serve (optional)

serves 2

Put the berries, yoghurt and milk in a blender and process for 1 minute until smooth. Put 1 tablespoon crushed ice, if using, in each of 2 tall glasses, then pour the smoothie over the top. Decorate the edge of the glasses with a couple of berries, if liked.

COOK'S TIP
• Frozen summer berries, defrosted, will work just as well and are as nutritious as fresh.

FULL OF FRUIT SMOOTHIE

PREPARATION TIME 10 minutes

1 small ripe mango, peeled, stone removed and flesh cut into small pieces

1 small ripe papaya, halved, deseeded and flesh cut into small pieces

2 ripe nectarines, halved and stones removed

4 slices fresh pineapple, peeled and cut into small pieces

120 ml freshly squeezed orange juice

2 tablespoons wheat bran

about 3 tablespoons crushed ice

serves 2

Put the fruit, orange juice and wheat bran in a blender and process to form a purée. Add 1 tablespoon crushed ice and blend again. Put 1 tablespoon crushed ice in each of 2 tall glasses, pour the smoothie over and serve.

GET UP 'N' GO SMOOTHIE

PREPARATION TIME 5–7 minutes

2 medium bananas, sliced

3 tablespoons smooth peanut butter

150 ml natural yoghurt

300 ml semi-skimmed milk, chilled (use whole milk for children under 5)

2 tablespoons crushed ice, to serve

serves 2

Put the bananas, peanut butter and yoghurt in a blender and process for about 1 minute until smooth.

Add the milk and process again until smooth. Put 1 tablespoon crushed ice in each of 2 tall glasses, pour the smoothie over and serve.

SESAME STREET

PREPARATION TIME 6–8 minutes

2 ripe melon wedges, about 100 g, seeds and skin removed and flesh chopped

100 g fresh or frozen raspberries, defrosted

2 medium bananas

1 tablespoon sesame seeds

1 tablespoon tahini (ground sesame seed paste)

300 ml semi-skimmed milk, chilled (use whole milk for children under 5)

1–2 teaspoons clear honey

serves 2

Put all the fruit in a blender and process to form a purée. Add 2 teaspoons sesame seeds and the tahini paste and process for 1 minute. With the motor running, gradually pour in the milk and honey and process until smooth. Pour the smoothie into 2 tall glasses, sprinkle with the remaining sesame seeds and serve.

LUNCH BOXES, SNACKS & DRINKS

LUNCH BOXES

Preparing children's lunch boxes can be a laborious task for busy parents. With little time to think about new variations, we tend to revert to the tried and tested formula of a sandwich, often with a high-fat filling, crisps, a shop-bought biscuit, a 'fruit' yoghurt, a carton of juice and the obligatory apple. Not only does this get repetitive for our kids, it also amounts to a lot of fat and sugar. In fact, a lunch such as this can contain more than 45 g of fat – approximately 80 per cent of the fat a child should eat in a day – and almost 11 teaspoons of sugar, more than a child's daily recommended amount.

SNACKS

Snacking on healthy foods between meals can be a great way of topping up energy levels. However, most commercially prepared snacks are extremely high in fat, salt, sugar and additives and sadly lacking in any real nutritional value. The more of these snacks children eat, the higher their intake of fat, salt, sugar and additives becomes and the less room there is for healthier foods like fruit and vegetables, resulting in serious short- and long-term health problems.

Savoury snacks are commonly seen as a healthier alternative to sweets because they appear to contain less sugar and are made from foods we perceive to be healthy, such as potatoes. In reality, they are often high in fat, especially saturated fat, and many contain artificial sweeteners and often very high levels of salt.

A recent survey that looked at the nutritional content of 283 commercially prepared snack foods found:

- The average snack had over 5 additives
- One-third contained colourings and 70 per cent contained flavourings or flavour enhancers
- One-fifth had high levels of hydrogenated fat
- One-quarter contained more than 30 per cent sugar; some had as much as 57 per cent
- Poor labelling and misleading health claims on packaging made it hard to make healthy choices
- Fifty-five per cent of crisps and snacks contained over twice the recommended level of saturated fat
- Crisps and savoury snacks had the highest levels of salt, with some 50 g portions providing over half the salt a child should eat in a day

DRINKS

Kids need to drink one to two litres of fluids a day to keep them fully hydrated. Insufficient fluids can result in headaches, reduced coordination, tiredness, a loss of stamina and an inability to concentrate. However, drinking healthily is as important as eating well.

Kids consume 30 times more soft drinks today than they did 50 years ago. Most squashes and fruit drinks contain very little fruit juice: they are mainly water and sugar (or artificial sweeteners) and are full of additives. Fizzy drinks have very few, if any, nutrients and a can of cola can contain up to 7 teaspoons of sugar, almost the maximum daily amount for a 6 year old.

SAVOURY SNACKS REAL ALTERNATIVES

mixed, unsalted nuts and raisins • green beans wrapped in Parma ham • oatcakes with cream cheese and grapes • celery filled with herby cream cheese • olives • sliced ham spread with hoummus and wrapped around carrot sticks • Cheddar cheese squares topped with grapes

SWEET SNACKS REAL ALTERNATIVES

chopped fresh fruit with nuts, seeds and sultanas • dry, home-made Muesli (page 32) and raisins • natural yoghurt with honey or fruit compote (page 121) • a stone fruit, such as a nectarine or plum • Chocolate-dipped Fruit (page 139)

DRINKS REAL ALTERNATIVES

add a small amount of fresh fruit juice, fresh mint leaves, crushed ice or orange or lemon slices to mineral water • add a little cordial to sparkling mineral water • freshly squeezed vegetable and fruit juices • home-made milkshakes (page 70) and smoothies (page 42) • hot milk and honey

HONEY ROASTED NUTS & SEEDS

Nuts and seeds are full of protein, vitamins, minerals and essential fatty acids. This snack has all this goodness without the high levels of saturated fat and salt of the shop-bought varieties.

PREPARATION TIME 3 minutes
COOKING TIME 10–15 minutes

500 g assorted whole skinned nuts, such as cashews, hazelnuts and almonds

225 g assorted seeds, such as sunflower and pumpkin

2 tablespoons clear honey

1 tablespoon shoyu or organic soy sauce

serves 8–10

Put the nuts and seeds in a roasting tin in an even layer. Cook in a preheated oven at 200°C (400°F) Gas 6 for 10–15 minutes, stirring occasionally, until golden brown.

Put the honey and shoyu or soy sauce in a bowl and mix well. As soon as the nuts are removed from the oven, pour the honey mixture over them and stir until thoroughly coated. Let cool completely before serving. Store in an airtight container for up to 1 week.

COOK'S TIP

- If you want to store the nuts and seeds for longer, roast them as in the main recipe, then let cool and store. To coat them, reheat the nuts for 5 minutes in a dry frying pan, stirring frequently, then pour over the honey mixture and stir until coated.

VEGETABLE CRISPS

These are a great way to increase your child's vegetable intake. However, they are fairly high in fat, so go easy.

PREPARATION TIME
25–30 minutes
COOKING TIME 30 minutes

1 beetroot

1 sweet potato

1 parsnip

1 large carrot

sunflower oil, for frying

serves 8–10

Peel all the vegetables. Using a vegetable peeler, preferably a swivel bladed one, peel very thin slices from the vegetables. Put some oil in a large saucepan or wok to a depth of 10 cm. Alternatively, fill a deep-fryer to the manufacturer's recommended level. Heat the oil to 160°C (325°F). Add batches of the thinly sliced vegetables to the hot oil (use a frying basket, if you have one) and blanch them for 1 minute until soft but not crisp. Remove the vegetable slices and drain well on kitchen paper. Repeat with the remaining vegetable slices.

Increase the temperature of the oil to 180°C (350°F) and fry a batch of the softened vegetable slices for about 1 minute until crisp. Remove and drain on kitchen paper. Repeat with the remaining vegetable slices. Let cool, then serve. Once cold, the crisps can be stored in an airtight container for up to 24 hours.

DIPS

Kids love dunking a stick of carrot or a chunk of bread into dips. Shop-bought dips can be okay, but read the label carefully to check that they aren't full of additives or overloaded with saturated fat and salt. These home-made dips are incredibly easy to make, packed with flavour and nutrients, and great for quick suppers, packed lunches or parties.

CREAMY GARLIC DIP

Garlic contains allicin, which has been shown to be particularly effective at strengthening the immune system, especially when eaten raw.

PREPARATION TIME 5 minutes

150 ml half fat crème fraîche

1–2 garlic cloves, crushed

1 tablespoon chopped fresh coriander

freshly ground black pepper

to serve

Vegetable Sticks (see below)

Bread Sticks (see below)

serves 4; makes 150 g

Put the crème fraîche, garlic, coriander and black pepper, to taste, in a small bowl and mix well. Serve with vegetable or bread sticks for dipping.

If not using immediately, cover tightly with clingfilm and store for up to 2 days in the refrigerator.

VARIATION
• Add 1 teaspoon curry paste or powder to the dip. Let stand for 30 minutes so the curry flavour can develop.

CRUNCHY DIP

Children that can weigh, measure and use a food processor will love making this dip. It's high in protein, calcium and omega 3 fatty acids.

PREPARATION TIME
5–8 minutes, plus cooling time
COOKING TIME
10–12 minutes

125 g sesame seeds

1 teaspoon coriander seeds

125 g skinned hazelnuts

1 teaspoon ground cumin

to serve

Vegetable Sticks (see right)

Creamy Garlic Dip (see above)

2 baking sheets

serves 8; makes 250 g

Put the seeds on one baking sheet and the hazelnuts on another. Cook the seeds in a preheated oven at 180°C (350°F) Gas 4 for 8–10 minutes until they begin to smell fragrant and look toasted. Cook the hazelnuts at the same temperature for 10–12 minutes or until golden brown.

Let cool slightly, then transfer the seeds and nuts to a food processor, using a funnel if necessary. Blend until finely crushed (don't blend for too long or they will turn to a paste). Stir in the ground cumin.

To serve, dip vegetable sticks into the Creamy Garlic Dip (or any of the dips on page 51), then into the toasted nuts and seeds. Store the crunchy dip in an airtight container in the refrigerator for up to 3 days.

DIPPERS

VEGETABLE STICKS
• Take any firm raw vegetables, such as carrots, cucumber, peppers, courgettes and celery. Wash thoroughly, peel if necessary, then cut into batons.
• Divide broccoli or cauliflower into tiny florets.
• Cut cherry tomatoes in half.
• Use baby sweetcorn or sugar snap peas.

BREAD STICKS
• Make 1 quantity Easy Peasy Wholemeal Bread dough (page 38). Divide the dough into small pieces, about the size of an apricot, then roll them in your hands to form thin sticks, about 10 cm long and 2 cm wide. Put them on a greased baking sheet and bake in a preheated oven at 230°C (450°F) Gas 8 for 8–10 minutes until lightly golden and crispy. Alternatively, toast a wholemeal pita bread and slice it into fingers.

GUACAMOLE

Avocados have the highest protein content of any fruit and are rich in mono-unsaturated fat (the type of fat that is linked with lowering the risk of heart disease, cancer and obesity). They are also a good source of vitamin C.

PREPARATION TIME
5–8 minutes

2 ripe avocados, peeled and stones removed

2 tablespoons freshly squeezed lemon or lime juice

2 ripe tomatoes

1 garlic clove, crushed

freshly ground black pepper

to serve

Vegetable Sticks (page 48)

Bread Sticks (page 48)

serves 4–6

Chop the avocados into small pieces and put them in a small bowl. Add the lemon or lime juice and toss well.

Cut the tomatoes into quarters and remove and discard the seeds, if you like. Put the tomatoes, garlic, avocado pieces and black pepper, to taste, in a food processor. Blend for 1–2 minutes until smooth. Transfer to a small serving bowl and serve with vegetable sticks and bread sticks for dipping.

If not using immediately, cover the bowl tightly with clingfilm and store in the refrigerator for up to 24 hours.

COOK'S TIP

• When choosing avocados to use immediately, select ones that are soft when touched but not squashy or badly discoloured on their skins. If buying a few days in advance, choose fruit that are firm and free from blemishes. Store at room temperature – they can discolour if stored in the refrigerator.

HOUMMUS

This dip contains lots of calcium and protein from the chickpeas and tahini, as well as iron, magnesium and fibre. It also has the immune-boosting power of garlic.

PREPARATION TIME 5–8 minutes

400 g canned chickpeas, rinsed and drained

2 tablespoons tahini (ground sesame seed paste)

2 tablespoons freshly squeezed lemon juice

2–3 tablespoons olive oil

1 garlic clove, crushed

to serve

Vegetable Sticks (page 48)

Bread Sticks (page 48)

serves 6–8

Put all the ingredients in a food processor and blend, using the pulse button, to form a smooth purée, about 1 minute. If the mixture is too stiff, add another tablespoon of oil and a little cooled boiled water. Serve with vegetable sticks or bread sticks for dipping.

If not using immediately, cover with clingfilm and store in the refrigerator for up to 3 days.

ROASTED ROOT DIPPERS

This is another great way to encourage your children to eat more vegetables.

PREPARATION TIME 10 minutes
COOKING TIME 40–50 minutes

1 sweet potato

1 parsnip

1 carrot

1 potato

2 tablespoons olive oil

a selection of dips, to serve

serves 4–6

Peel the vegetables and cut them into thick, chunky chips. Put them in a roasting tin, pour over the oil and toss well to coat.

Roast in a preheated oven at 190°C (375°F) Gas 5 for 40–50 minutes, stirring occasionally, until the vegetables are tender. Serve immediately with dips of your choice.

SMOKED TROUT PÂTÉ

Trout is an oily fish and is therefore a great source of omega 3 fatty acids, which promote healthy brain development and help reduce the risk of heart disease in later life.

PREPARATION TIME
12–15 minutes

150 g smoked trout fillets

100 g cream cheese

1–2 tablespoons freshly squeezed lemon juice

1 tablespoon chopped fresh dill

freshly ground black pepper

to serve

dill sprigs

pita bread, toasted

serves 4–6

Remove any fine bones from the trout fillets, then break them up into tiny pieces.

Put the cream cheese and 1 tablespoon lemon juice in a small bowl and beat with a wooden spoon until soft and creamy. Stir in the trout, dill and pepper, to taste. Add more lemon juice, if necessary, to give a spreading consistency. Cover with clingfilm and chill in the refrigerator for 30 minutes.

To serve, sprinkle with dill sprigs and accompany with toasted pita bread.

Store, covered, in the refrigerator for up to 2 days.

Did You Know?

A diet rich in omega 3 and omega 6 fatty acids – found in oily fish, nuts and seeds – may improve the behavioural patterns of children with attention deficit disorder.

VEGETABLE & NUT PÂTÉ

Nuts and seeds are full of protein and brain-boosting, immune-strengthening essential fatty acids. This recipe combines them with carrots, celery and leeks to make a really nutritious pâté.

PREPARATION TIME 12–15 minutes
COOKING TIME 15 minutes

1 celery stick, finely chopped

1 small carrot, finely chopped

1 small leek, finely chopped

1 small onion, finely chopped

50 g sunflower seeds

50 g hazelnuts

5 medium closed cup mushrooms

1 garlic clove, crushed

1 teaspoon organic vegetable bouillon powder made up to 50 ml stock

freshly ground black pepper

Vegetable Sticks or Bread Sticks (page 48), to serve

serves 6–8

Put the celery, carrot, leek and onion in a steamer over a pan of gently simmering water and steam for 15 minutes until soft. Remove from the heat and let cool slightly.

Meanwhile, put the sunflower seeds and hazelnuts in a food processor and blend until finely ground. Remove and set aside.

Transfer the vegetables to the food processor, add the mushrooms and garlic and, using the pulse button, blend until a purée is formed.

Add the ground sunflower seeds and hazelnuts, bouillon and black pepper and blend again until thoroughly mixed. Spoon into a small bowl, cover and chill in the refrigerator for 30 minutes.

Serve with vegetable sticks or bread sticks.

SMOKED SALMON & CREAM CHEESE BAGEL

PREPARATION TIME 10–12 minutes

4 sesame seed bagels, halved

2–3 tablespoons half fat cream cheese

4 thin slices smoked salmon, about 100 g

5 cm piece cucumber, sliced

2 tablespoons Coleslaw (page 59), optional

serves 4

Spread all the bagel halves with the cream cheese. Put a slice of smoked salmon and some cucumber slices on four of the bagel halves. Divide the coleslaw, if using, between them, then top with the bagel lids.

Cut each bagel in half. Wrap in non-pvc food wrap or foil and store in the refrigerator until ready to pack.

VARIATIONS

- Vegetable and Nut Pâté (page 52) with shredded lettuce.
- Cream cheese topped with halved grapes.
- Vegetable Burger (page 109) with a little Salsa (page 96) or sliced tomato.
- Thinly sliced organic ham with cream cheese and a spread of Walnut Pesto (page 86).

HOUMMUS PITA POCKETS

PREPARATION TIME 15 minutes

4 wholemeal pita breads

4 tablespoons Hoummus (page 51)

½ Cos lettuce, roughly shredded

8 cm piece cucumber, thinly sliced

3–4 medium tomatoes, thinly sliced

1 carrot, grated

25 g half fat Cheddar cheese, grated

serves 4

Warm the pita breads in a toaster or under a hot grill for 1 minute. Let cool slightly, then split them. Put 1 tablespoon hoummus in each one. Half fill with lettuce, then add some cucumber and tomato slices and grated carrot. Add some cheese, then wrap in non-pvc food wrap or foil and store in the refrigerator until ready to pack.

CHICKEN & AVOCADO ROLL

PREPARATION TIME 12–15 minutes

1 large avocado, peeled, stone removed and flesh sliced

2 teaspoons freshly squeezed lemon juice

1 medium tomato, deseeded and finely chopped

4 wholemeal rolls, halved

2–3 tablespoons low fat cream cheese

1 Little Gem lettuce, rinsed

100 g thinly sliced roast organic chicken

serves 4

Put the avocado slices and lemon juice in a small bowl and mash to a rough purée with a fork. Add the tomato and mix well.

Spread each half of the rolls with a little cream cheese. Put a couple of lettuce leaves and 1–2 slices of chicken on top of 4 of the halves. Top with a spoonful of the avocado mixture and put the bread lid on top. Press lightly together, then wrap in non-pvc food wrap or foil and store in the refrigerator until ready to pack.

SALADS

These salads are delicious, packed with nutrients and a great alternative to sandwiches. They also make excellent suppers. On those really busy days when you don't have time to think, why not make a large salad for supper and set some aside for lunch the next day?

TUNA PASTA SALAD

PREPARATION TIME
15–20 minutes
COOKING TIME
12–15 minutes

100 g wholewheat pasta, such as penne

1 red onion, thinly sliced

3 celery stalks, chopped

1 carrot, grated

50 g sultanas

8 cm piece cucumber, chopped

50 g cooked sweetcorn kernels

400 g canned tuna in spring water, drained and flaked

6 tablespoons reduced calorie mayonnaise

6 tablespoons Greek yoghurt

to serve

salad leaves

225 g small vine-ripened plum tomatoes, halved

serves 4–6

Cook the pasta in a large saucepan of boiling water for 12–15 minutes, or according to the instructions on the packet, until 'al dente' (cooked but with a slight bite to it). Drain, refresh under cold running water and transfer to a large bowl.

Cut the onion slices in half to form half moons, then add to the bowl along with the celery, carrot, sultanas, cucumber, sweetcorn and tuna.

Mix the mayonnaise with the yoghurt and add it to the salad. Stir gently until well coated. (You can make the recipe up to this point and store, covered, in the refrigerator for up to 2 days.)

To serve, line a lunch box or airtight container with the salad leaves, put a serving of the pasta salad on top and scatter over a few halved tomatoes.

COUSCOUS SALAD

Every busy parent should keep a packet of couscous in the cupboard. It couldn't be quicker or easier to prepare, it can be eaten hot or cold in a number of different ways and children really like its texture.

PREPARATION TIME 15–18 minutes

350 g pre-cooked couscous

1 red pepper, deseeded and chopped

1 yellow pepper, deseeded and chopped

500 g vine ripened tomatoes, finely chopped

8 cm piece cucumber, finely chopped

50 g raisins

50 g pecan nuts, toasted

50 g black olives, pitted and halved

2 tablespoons chopped fresh flat leaf parsley

2 tablespoons chopped fresh mint leaves

3 tablespoons extra virgin olive oil

2 tablespoons freshly squeezed lemon juice

1 teaspoon clear honey, warmed

1 tablespoon balsamic vinegar

freshly ground black pepper

serves 4–6

Put the couscous in a large heatproof bowl and cover with 250 ml boiling water. Stir, cover and let stand for 10 minutes.

Fluff up the couscous with a fork. Add the peppers, tomatoes, cucumber, raisins, pecans, olives and herbs and mix well. (You can make the recipe up to this point and store, covered, in the refrigerator for up to 2 days.)

Put the oil, lemon juice, honey, vinegar and pepper in a screw-top jar and shake until well mixed. Pour it over the couscous and stir well. Transfer to a lunch box or airtight container.

SAFFRON FISH PILAFF

This protein-packed salad uses basmati rice which has the added advantage of releasing its sugars into the blood stream at a very slow rate throughout the afternoon.

PREPARATION TIME
15 minutes
COOKING TIME 45 minutes

2 teaspoons virgin olive oil

1 onion, chopped

2–3 garlic cloves, crushed (optional)

175 g brown basmati rice, rinsed

¼ teaspoon saffron powder

750–900 ml vegetable stock

350 g white fish, such as cod loin, skinned if necessary and cut into small pieces

100 g undyed smoked haddock fillet, skinned and cut into small pieces (optional)

50 g frozen peas

50 g frozen sweetcorn kernels

225 g tomatoes, chopped

1 tablespoon chopped fresh coriander

2 hard boiled eggs, shelled and quartered (page 41)

freshly ground black pepper

serves 4–6

Heat the oil in a large frying pan, add the onion and garlic, if using, and fry gently for 3 minutes. Add the rice and continue to fry, stirring, for 2 minutes. Add the saffron powder and stir well. Pour in half the stock, bring to the boil, then reduce the heat and simmer gently for 25 minutes, stirring occasionally, adding more stock as it is absorbed by the rice.

Add the fish, peas, sweetcorn and tomatoes, stir well and cook for a further 5–10 minutes. Add the coriander and black pepper, to taste, then cook for 5 minutes more until the rice is tender.

Top with the hard boiled egg, then transfer to an airtight container or a lunch box.

VARIATION
• Replace the fish with 300 g chopped ham and 100 g chopped fresh pineapple.

COLESLAW

Shop-bought coleslaw tends to contain (amongst other things) the minimum amount of vegetables and lots of high fat, watered down mayonnaise. This home-made version is quite the opposite. It is so full of fruit and vegetables that it is almost a main course in itself. The walnuts add extra protein and essential fatty acids.

PREPARATION TIME 20 minutes

2 red apples, about 175 g

4 tablespoons freshly squeezed orange or lemon juice

450 g white cabbage

1 onion, thinly sliced or grated

175 g carrots, grated

3 celery sticks, finely chopped

50 g sultanas

50 g walnuts, chopped (optional)

6 tablespoons half fat crème fraîche

freshly ground black pepper

serves 4–6

Quarter and core the apples, then grate them into a large bowl, add 2 tablespoons of the orange or lemon juice and stir until well coated.

Cut the cabbage into wedges and discard the outer leaves and hard central core. Wash thoroughly, then shred finely. (Use the shredding attachment on a food processor to save time.) Add it to the apple along with the onion, carrots, celery, sultanas and walnuts, if using. Stir well.

In a separate bowl, mix the crème fraîche with the remaining orange or lemon juice and pepper, to taste. Add it to the vegetables and stir well. The coleslaw can be stored in an airtight container in the refrigerator for up to 2 days.

VARIATION
• Try adding sweetcorn kernels, shredded red and green pepper and grated celeriac to the mixture.

OATY CHOCOLATE CRUNCHIES

There is nothing wrong with a little chocolate now and again, especially when it's high in iron-rich cocoa solids and melted over nutritious nuts, seeds and oats.

PREPARATION TIME
10–12 minutes

100 g plain chocolate (at least 70 per cent cocoa solids)

225 g Granola (page 32)

12 paper cake cases

makes 12

Break the chocolate into small pieces and put them in a heatproof bowl. Place the bowl over a saucepan of gently simmering, not boiling, water. Make sure the bottom of the bowl doesn't touch the water. Melt the chocolate gently, stirring occasionally, until it is smooth. Remove the bowl from the pan.

Add the granola to the melted chocolate and mix thoroughly. Put about 1 tablespoon of the mixture into each paper case. Leave for 1 hour until set before serving. Store in an airtight container for up to 1 week.

Did You Know?

Chocolate with a high cocoa solid content (at least 70 per cent) contains immune-boosting antioxidants, as well as more iron and twice the magnesium levels of milk chocolate. It also triggers the release of serotonin and endorphin, which make us feel happier. But go easy, because despite its good points, chocolate is still high in fat.

APRICOT & WALNUT FLAPJACK

These flapjacks are much lower in fat than most shop-bought versions. The dried apricots and oats make them high in fibre and very filling. The walnuts add a lovely extra crunch as well as protein and omega 3 fatty acids.

PREPARATION TIME 12 minutes
COOKING TIME 20–25 minutes

100 g sunflower margarine

2 tablespoons light muscovado sugar

5 tablespoons golden syrup

200 g porridge oats

75 g ready-to-eat dried apricots, chopped

50 g walnuts, chopped

a baking tin, 18 cm square, lightly greased

serves 10

Put the margarine, sugar and golden syrup in a large saucepan and heat gently, stirring occasionally, until the margarine has melted and the sugar has dissolved.

Remove the pan from the heat and add the oats, apricots and walnuts. Stir well until thoroughly mixed, then press into the prepared baking tin with the back of a spoon.

Bake in a preheated oven at 180°C (350°F) Gas 4 for 20–25 minutes until golden and firm to the touch. Remove from the oven and let cool before cutting into bars. Leave until completely cold before removing from the tin. Store in an airtight container for up to 5 days.

GINGERBREAD PEOPLE

Younger children will love to help you make these. They will be far lower in saturated fat, sugar and additives than most biscuits you are likely to buy at the supermarket. Ground ginger is rich in iron as are the ground almonds, which are also high in calcium and magnesium (both needed for strong bone development) and zinc, which supports the immune system and builds resistance to disease.

PREPARATION TIME 20 minutes

COOKING TIME 10–12 minutes

200 g self-raising flour

½ teaspoon bicarbonate of soda

1–2 teaspoons ground ginger

2 teaspoons light muscovado sugar

1 tablespoon ground almonds

50 g sunflower margarine

75 g golden syrup

currants, for decorating

shaped pastry cutter

2–3 baking sheets, lightly greased

makes 12

Sift the flour, bicarbonate of soda and ground ginger into a large bowl. Stir in the sugar and ground almonds.

Melt the margarine and golden syrup in a heavy based saucepan over gentle heat, stirring occasionally, until melted. Remove the pan from the heat and gradually add to the flour, mixing with a wooden spoon, to give a soft but not sticky dough. Knead gently just to bring the dough together.

Transfer the dough to a lightly floured work surface and roll out to a thickness of 4 mm. Using a shaped pastry cutter, cut out people shapes, then carefully lift them onto a baking sheet using a spatula. Press in a few currants for buttons, then mark the mouth and eyes with a small sharp knife.

Bake in a preheated oven at 190°C (375°F) Gas 5 for 10–12 minutes until golden brown. Let cool for 5 minutes on the baking sheets, then transfer them carefully to a wire rack and let cool completely. Store in an airtight container for up to 1 week.

CHOCOLATE CHIP & OATMEAL BISCUITS

Oatmeal is high in a number of minerals including zinc, iron, calcium and magnesium. It is also a good source of B vitamins, needed for everything from energy production to good brain function and the healthy development of nerve tissues. The combination of the oatmeal and the wholemeal flour will ensure that the sugars from this snack are released into the blood stream at a slow, steady and sustained pace.

PREPARATION TIME 12–15 minutes

COOKING TIME 12–15 minutes

100 g wholemeal self-raising flour

100 g medium oatmeal

40 g light muscovado sugar

85 g raisins

50 g plain chocolate (at least 70 per cent cocoa solids), finely chopped

1 egg

2 tablespoons sunflower oil

2–3 tablespoons milk

2 baking sheets, lightly greased

makes 12–14

Put the flour and oatmeal in a large bowl and stir in the sugar, raisins and chocolate. Put the egg in a small bowl and beat in the oil and milk. Stir the egg mixture into the flour and mix to form a stiff dough.

Put small spoonfuls of the mixture on the baking sheets, spacing them well apart. Flatten slightly with the prongs of a fork, then bake in a preheated oven at 180°C (350°F) Gas 4 for 12–15 minutes until golden.

Let cool on the baking sheets for 2–3 minutes, then transfer to a wire rack and let cool completely. The biscuits can be stored in an airtight container for up to 5 days.

EASY CARROT CAKE CUPS

These are a firm favourite with my children and they couldn't be easier to make. The nuts add an irresistible crunch to what is otherwise a really moist, soft cake.

PREPARATION TIME 15 minutes
COOKING TIME 15–25 minutes

2 eggs

100 g caster sugar

225 g grated carrot

100 ml freshly squeezed orange juice

2 teaspoons finely grated unwaxed orange zest

100 g pecans or walnuts, roughly chopped

½ teaspoon ground cinnamon

120 ml sunflower oil

300 g self-raising flour, sifted

topping (optional)

200 g cream cheese

1 tablespoon finely grated unwaxed lemon zest

225 g icing sugar

a 12-hole muffin tin, lined with 9 paper muffin cases

makes 9 cakes

Put the eggs, sugar, carrot, orange juice and zest, nuts, cinnamon, oil and flour in a large bowl and stir with a wooden spoon until well mixed.

Spoon the mixture into the paper cases, until three-quarters full. Bake in a preheated oven at 180°C (350°F) Gas 4 for 40 minutes until cooked. Test by inserting a clean skewer into the centre of a cake; it should come out clean. Remove from the oven and let cool.

To make the topping, if using, put the cream cheese and lemon zest in a bowl and beat with a wooden spoon until soft. Gradually beat in the icing sugar to form a stiff icing. Spread on top of the cooled cakes. Store in an airtight container for up to 3 days.

DOUBLE CHOCOLATE & HAZELNUT BROWNIES

Everyone loves chocolate brownies. These use sunflower margarine instead of butter to lower the saturated fat content, cocoa powder and plain chocolate to boost the iron content and chopped hazelnuts to increase the amount of essential fatty acids and minerals. Serve as a tea-time treat, in packed lunches, at parties or as a pudding with fresh raspberries.

PREPARATION TIME
12–15 minutes
COOKING TIME 25 minutes

100 g plain chocolate (at least 70 per cent cocoa solids)

2 tablespoons milk

125 g sunflower margarine

200 g unrefined caster sugar

2 eggs, beaten

50 g unsweetened cocoa powder

75 g self-raising flour

50 g chopped hazelnuts

a baking tin, 18 cm square, lightly greased and completely lined with non-stick baking parchment

makes 9 squares

Break the chocolate into small pieces and put in a heavy based saucepan. Add the milk and heat gently, stirring, until the chocolate is melted and smooth. Remove the pan from the heat and let cool slightly.

Put the margarine and sugar in a large bowl and beat with a hand-held electric mixer or a wooden spoon until the mixture is light and fluffy. Beat in the eggs a little at a time, beating well after each addition, until blended. Sift the cocoa powder into the egg mixture and stir gently until mixed. Pour in the melted chocolate and stir well.

Gently stir in the flour and hazelnuts – do not beat or overmix or the brownies will be dry. Spoon the mixture into the prepared tin and smooth the top. Bake in a preheated oven at 160°C (325°F) Gas 3 for about 25 minutes. To test if they are cooked, insert a skewer into the centre; it should come out almost clean with a slightly sticky feel.

Remove from the oven and let cool before marking into squares. Store in an airtight container for up to 1 week, or wrap and freeze for up to 1 month.

APPLE TEA BREAD

This tea bread is so versatile. It is great eaten just as it is for picnics or car journeys, but it is also delicious served as a quick snack with some Cheddar cheese and halved grapes on top. Alternatively, serve it warm for pudding topped with a little half fat crème fraîche.

PREPARATION TIME
15 minutes
COOKING TIME
45–50 minutes

280 g wholemeal self-raising flour

125 g light muscovado sugar

1 teaspoon baking powder, sifted

1 teaspoon ground cinnamon

½ teaspoon freshly grated nutmeg

180 g apple, cored and grated

75 g sultanas

50 g walnuts, chopped

100 g unsalted butter, melted

1 egg, beaten

about 80 ml clear apple juice

a loaf tin, 900 g, lightly greased and lined with non-stick baking parchment

makes 1 loaf

Put the flour, sugar, baking powder and spices in a large bowl and mix. Stir in the grated apple, sultanas and walnuts. Mix well.

Mix in the melted butter, then stir in the beaten egg and the apple juice to give a soft dropping consistency. Add a little more apple juice if the mixture is too stiff.

Spoon the mixture into the prepared tin and bake in a preheated oven at 180°C (350°F) Gas 4 for 45–50 minutes until cooked. To check, insert a skewer into the centre of the loaf; it should come out clean. Remove from the oven and let cool in the tin. Serve in slices. Store in an airtight container for up to 5 days, or wrap and freeze for up to 1 month.

DATE BARS

Dates are naturally sweet and yet they will release their sugars at a far slower, steadier pace into the blood stream than other more refined sugars.

PREPARATION TIME
12–15 minutes
COOKING TIME
25–30 minutes

350 g pitted dates

175 g wholemeal flour

175 g porridge oats

175 g sunflower margarine

a baking tin, 18 cm square, lightly greased and lined with non-stick baking parchment

makes 9

Put the dates and 225 ml cold water in a heavy based saucepan and bring to the boil. Reduce the heat and simmer gently for 5–8 minutes until the dates are very soft. Beat with a wooden spoon or transfer to a blender and process to form a purée. Let cool.

Sift the flour into a large bowl and stir in the oats. Add the sunflower margarine and rub in with the tips of your fingers until the mixture resembles fine breadcrumbs. Add 3–4 tablespoons cold water and mix with a round-bladed knife to form a soft dough.

Put half the dough in the prepared tin and press out to cover the base. Spread the date purée over the top. Put the remaining dough on top and press out carefully to cover the dates. Bake in a preheated oven at 190°C (375°F) Gas 5 for 25–30 minutes until golden. Remove from the oven and let cool before marking into 9 squares. Once cold, cut out the squares and remove them from the tin. Store in an airtight container for up to 1 week.

FRESH FRUIT DRINKS

All too often shop-bought drinks and cordials are laden with sugar to give them taste, additives to give them shelf life and colourings to give them 'child appeal'. These recipes use the natural sugars and colours of fresh fruit and vegetables instead and they're packed with naturally occurring vitamins and minerals.

PEAR & GINGER JUICE

Pear is very gentle on the digestive system and ginger is an effective remedy against nausea and travel sickness, so this is a great drink to take on journeys or to give to your child after a stomach upset.

PREPARATION TIME 5 minutes

350 g ripe pears, peeled, cored and chopped

1 large orange, broken into segments

2 cm piece ginger, chopped

2 tablespoons crushed ice, to serve (optional)

serves 2

Push the pears, orange and ginger through a juicer. Put 1 tablespoon crushed ice, if using, in each of 2 tall glasses, pour the juice over the top and serve.

APPLE & CARROT JUICE

This is high in soluble fibre, which is necessary for a healthy digestive system, and full of immune-boosting antioxidants.

PREPARATION TIME
8 minutes

3 medium carrots, chopped

2 eating apples, peeled, cored and chopped

2 tablespoons crushed ice, to serve (optional)

serves 2

Push the carrot and apple pieces through a juicer. Put 1 tablespoon crushed ice, if using, in each of 2 tall glasses, pour the juice over the top and serve.

LEMON CORDIAL

Packed with vitamin C, this is a great immune-boosting drink.

PREPARATION TIME
15 minutes

freshly squeezed juice and zest of 6 unwaxed lemons

450 g unrefined granulated sugar

to serve

lemon slices

ice cubes (optional)

makes 2 litres

Put the lemon juice in a large bowl, add the sugar and stir well.

Put the lemon zest and 1.2 litres cold water in a saucepan and bring to the boil. Reduce the heat and simmer for 3 minutes. Strain through a fine mesh strainer onto the lemon juice and sugar mixture and stir until the sugar has dissolved. Discard the zest.

Cover loosely and let cool completely. Pour the cordial into 2 sterilized screw-top bottles (page 4) and close securely.

To serve, pour a small amount of cordial into a tall glass and dilute to taste with cold water. Add slices of lemon and ice cubes, if liked.

Store in the refrigerator for up to 2 weeks.

MILKSHAKES

Milkshakes are almost an entire meal in themselves and provide the perfect opportunity to increase your child's fruit intake. Here are a few delicious ideas that can be whizzed up in minutes. Don't be afraid to experiment by adding any type of soft fruit that you know your child likes.

CHOCOLATE MONKEY MILKSHAKE

Bananas are the perfect fast food. They are satisfyingly filling, release their sugars slowly into the blood stream and are high in potassium and vitamin B6.

PREPARATION TIME
5 minutes

300 ml semi-skimmed milk (use whole milk for children under 5)

150 ml natural yoghurt

2 ripe bananas, sliced

2 tablespoons crushed ice (optional)

2 teaspoons finely grated plain chocolate (at least 70 per cent cocoa solids)

serves 2

Put the milk, yoghurt and bananas in a blender and process until smooth. Put 1 tablespoon crushed ice, if using, in each of 2 tall glasses and pour the milkshake over the top. Sprinkle with the grated chocolate and serve immediately.

HONEY, APPLE & BANANA SHAKE

PREPARATION TIME 5 minutes

2 ripe bananas, sliced

250 ml natural yoghurt

2 teaspoons clear honey

200 ml clear apple juice

ice cubes, to serve (optional)

serves 2

Put the bananas, yoghurt, honey and apple juice in a blender and process until smooth. Pour into 2 tall glasses, add ice cubes, if using, and serve immediately.

RASPBERRY MILKSHAKE

PREPARATION TIME 5 minutes

150 ml semi-skimmed milk (use whole milk for children under 5)

125 ml natural yoghurt

50 g raspberries

2 teaspoons high fruit content raspberry jam (optional)

2 tablespoons crushed ice, to serve

serves 2

Put the milk, yoghurt, raspberries and jam, if using, in a blender and process for 1 minute. Put 1 tablespoon crushed ice in each of 2 tall glasses and pour in the milkshake. Serve immediately.

VARIATION
- Use pitted canned black cherries or fresh blackberries or strawberries in place of the raspberries.

Did You Know?
Raspberries contain ellagic acid which is known to help protect against cancer. They are also packed with vitamin C.

LUNCHES & SUPPERS

THE MAIN MEAL OF THE DAY

The food industry spends millions of pounds each year convincing both us and our children that the foods they produce are nutritious and desirable. Consequently, fish fingers, burgers, baked beans, chicken nuggets, pizza and chips have become the staple foods on offer to our children, whether it's at home, in restaurants, nurseries or schools. The high fat, salt and sugar content of these foods makes them a delight to a child's taste buds and they are therefore readily accepted. This only serves to confirm the belief that kids need to eat these foods. However, a closer look at the content and nutritional value of these products shows that nothing could be further from the truth.

FISH FINGERS Fresh fish coated in breadcrumbs or a little batter sounds a healthy choice. However, many versions contain unrecognizable fish pulp made from fish scraps, which is blended with salt and other additives, then reformed into the shape of a fish finger. These are then coated in breadcrumbs or batter, which may also contain additives and only serves to increase the fat content.

BURGERS AND SAUSAGES A recent report by The Food Commission found that most frozen burgers are fatty, over-salted products pumped up with non-meat fillers, water and flavourings. Some burgers contain 6 teaspoons of artery clogging saturated fat – even after being grilled. The survey also found many companies used cheap filling agents to pad out the meat, and chemicals to increase the amount of water in the product. The same is true of many sausages.

Burgers and sausages, especially the cheaper varieties, are often made from the very last scraps of meat from a carcass that can legally be used.

CHICKEN NUGGETS The meat used in chicken nuggets is invariably low-grade mulch from intensively produced poultry, bound with chemical additives and cheap fillers. The coating retains the fat from the meat, even if the nuggets are grilled. Some varieties have been found to contain only one-third meat and two-thirds coating.

PIZZA Most commercially prepared pizzas consist of a highly refined dough base topped with over-sweetened tomato paste, processed cheese and the occasional slice of very salty, additive-packed processed meat. They are often devoid of vegetables and, although filling, offer very little nutritional value.

CHIPS Deep-fried chips are very high in fat. Even oven chips can contain up to 40 per cent fat, even when the label declares there is only 5 per cent. This is because manufacturers measure fat in terms of weight rather than calories, which is ludicrous as our bodies metabolize calories not grams.

BAKED BEANS The beans themselves contain fibre, protein and other valuable vitamins. However, most commercially prepared baked beans are coated in a sauce that is excessively high in both sugar and salt.

READY MEALS Although very convenient to buy, the nutritional content of ready meals is often very low. Much of the food's natural flavour is lost during processing, so extra fat, salt and sugar are often added. The shelf life is prolonged with preservatives and the appearance enhanced with colourings.

REAL ALTERNATIVES
wholemeal spaghetti mixed with peas and sweetcorn, a chopped fresh tomato, a little olive oil and some grated Cheddar cheese sprinkled over • Dippy Eggs (page 41) with wholemeal toast • Home-made Baked Beans (page 76) mixed with canned mackerel, served on wholemeal toast • blend a can of chopped tomatoes with a can of tuna and a can of butter beans, heat and serve with crusty wholemeal bread • boiled egg, bacon and tomato on toast • add some frozen mixed vegetables to a saucepan of boiling pasta a couple of minutes before the pasta is cooked, drain and mix with some pesto and half fat crème fraîche • toast a wholemeal pita bread and fill with sliced avocado and tomato and organic sliced ham • heat a flour tortilla and fill with mashed avocado, shredded chicken, some half fat crème fraîche and chopped tomato

CREAMY POTATO & BROCCOLI SOUP

Broccoli is one of the best cancer-fighting vegetables you can eat. It is also packed with immune-boosting phytochemicals and is an excellent source of vitamin C and beta-carotene.

PREPARATION TIME 12–15 minutes
COOKING TIME about 30 minutes

1 tablespoon olive oil

1 large onion, chopped

2 garlic cloves, crushed

400 g potatoes, cut into 2.5 cm cubes

750 ml vegetable stock

500 g broccoli, divided into florets and chopped

100–150 ml semi-skimmed milk (use whole milk for children under 5)

freshly ground black pepper

serves 4

Heat the olive oil in a large, heavy based saucepan. Add the onion and garlic and fry gently for 5–8 minutes until soft but not browned. Add the cubed potatoes and cook for a further 3 minutes.

Pour in the stock, bring to the boil, cover with a lid and simmer for 15 minutes. Add the broccoli and cook for a further 5–8 minutes until the vegetables are soft. Remove from the heat and let cool slightly.

Transfer the contents of the pan to a blender or food processor and blend, in batches if necessary, to form a smooth purée. Return the purée to the rinsed pan and stir in sufficient milk to give a slightly thick soup. Add pepper to taste and reheat gently, stirring occasionally, until hot. Ladle into warm soup bowls to serve.

PUMPKIN SOUP

This is a really filling, warming soup that is perfect for chilly autumn days. It is packed full of beta-carotene, a powerful antioxidant that will boost the immune system as well as lower the risk of many cancers. Pumpkin is also easy to digest, so it's great for kids recovering from short bouts of illness.

PREPARATION TIME
15–18 minutes
COOKING TIME
about 30 minutes

1 pumpkin, about 1 kg

1 tablespoon olive oil

1 potato, about 200 g, diced

1 onion, chopped

1–2 garlic cloves, crushed

1 teaspoon ground cumin

900 ml vegetable or chicken stock

1 tablespoon chopped fresh sage leaves

150 ml half fat crème fraîche

to serve, your choice of:

freshly grated nutmeg

finely grated Gruyère or Cheddar cheese

roasted pumpkin seeds (see cook's tips)

croutons (see cook's tips)

serves 6

Using a large sharp knife, cut the pumpkin into small wedges, then scoop out the seeds (see cook's tips). Using a small sharp vegetable knife, peel and discard the skin then cut the flesh into small pieces.

Heat the oil in a heavy based saucepan, add the potato, onion and garlic and cook gently, stirring occasionally, for 5–8 minutes until the vegetables are softened but not browned. Sprinkle in the ground cumin and cook for 1 minute more.

Add the stock, chopped pumpkin and sage to the pan. Bring to the boil, reduce the heat, cover and simmer gently for 20–25 minutes until the pumpkin is soft.

Remove the pan from the heat and let cool slightly. Transfer the mixture to a blender or food processor and blend, in batches if necessary, to form a smooth purée.

Return the purée to the rinsed pan and heat gently. Stir in the crème fraîche, then ladle into warm soup bowls. Serve sprinkled with a little freshly grated nutmeg, some grated cheese, roasted pumpkin seeds or croutons.

COOK'S TIPS

- To roast the pumpkin seeds, first rinse them, discarding any pith around them. Spread them out in an even layer on a baking sheet and let dry. Roast in a preheated oven at 190°C (375°F) Gas 5 for 10–15 minutes, stirring occasionally, until golden.
- To make croutons, cut 2 slices of wholemeal bread into small cubes. Heat 2 tablespoons olive oil in a heavy based frying pan, add the bread cubes and cook over moderate heat, stirring frequently, for 5–8 minutes until golden and crisp. Drain on kitchen paper.

SARDINE BRUSCHETTA

These Italian-inspired toasted sandwiches are extremely versatile and make a delicious and quick lunch or supper dish.

PREPARATION TIME 5 minutes
COOKING TIME 2–3 minutes

120 g canned sardines

1 teaspoon balsamic vinegar

1 slice of wholemeal bread, lightly toasted

1 tablespoon finely grated Cheddar cheese (optional)

3–4 cherry tomatoes, halved

serves 1

Put the sardines and balsamic vinegar in a bowl and mash with a fork. Pile the sardines on top of the toasted bread and sprinkle with the grated cheese, if using.

Transfer to a grill rack along with the tomatoes and cook under a preheated grill for 2–3 minutes until the cheese is golden brown and the tomatoes are hot.

Put the tomatoes on top of the toast, cut it into fingers and serve immediately.

HOME-MADE BAKED BEANS

Ready prepared baked beans are so cheap to buy that it may seem like madness to make your own. Until you inspect the label, that is. Most commercially prepared versions are extremely high in salt and sugar. Some cans contain as many as 4 teaspoons of sugar, and almost twice as much salt as a young child should eat in a whole day.

PREPARATION TIME 10 minutes
COOKING TIME 1–1¼ hours

1.7 kg canned beans, such as haricot, cannellini or borlotti, rinsed and drained

3 medium onions, finely chopped

4 garlic cloves, crushed

2 tablespoons olive oil

1–1½ teaspoons paprika

1½–2 tablespoons molasses or dark muscovado sugar

3 tablespoons tomato purée

4 teaspoons Worcestershire sauce (optional)

sea salt and freshly ground black pepper

toasted wholemeal bread, to serve

a large casserole

serves 15–20

Put the beans in a large casserole, add all the remaining ingredients (except the toast), season lightly with salt and pepper and cover with 500 ml boiling water. Mix well.

Cover and cook in a preheated oven at 180°C (350°F) Gas 4 for 1–1¼ hours, stirring occasionally, until the sauce is thick and rich in taste and texture. Check the seasoning; add extra Worcestershire sauce, if necessary, and extra molasses if slightly bitter.

Serve immediately on freshly toasted wholemeal bread.

COOK'S TIPS
- This may seem like a large quantity to make, but the beans freeze well. To freeze, let cool, then transfer to freezerproof containers. Freeze for up to 1 month.
- These beans would make an ideal accompaniment for grilled fish, chicken or burgers (pages 106–109), or serve them on top of a baked sweet potato.

VARIATIONS
- Add some chopped fresh parsley or coriander at the end of cooking.
- Add ½ teaspoon chilli powder with the rest of the ingredients.
- Add some chopped grilled bacon, ham or sliced premium-quality sausage towards the end of cooking and ensure that the meat or sausage is thoroughly cooked and piping hot before serving.

FRITTATA

PREPARATION TIME 5–8 minutes

COOKING TIME 15 minutes

50 g baby spinach leaves

50 g frozen peas

50 g frozen sweetcorn

6 eggs

1 tablespoon olive oil

1 medium onion, thinly sliced

3 ripe tomatoes, finely chopped

1 tablespoon chopped fresh flat leaf parsley

sea salt and freshly ground black pepper

to serve

salad leaves

wholegrain bread

a non-stick frying pan, 23 cm diameter

serves 4

Rinse the spinach, drain well, then put it in a saucepan with only the water clinging to the leaves. Cook over medium heat for 2–3 minutes until just wilted. Drain well, squeezing out any excess water, then chop it finely.

Put the frozen peas and sweetcorn in a saucepan of simmering water and cook for 3 minutes. Drain.

Put the eggs and 3 tablespoons cold water in a bowl and beat well. Add salt and pepper to taste, then stir in the drained spinach.

Heat the oil in the frying pan, add the onion and fry gently for about 5 minutes, stirring frequently, until it is softened but not browned. Pour the egg mixture into the pan and cook over medium heat for 3 minutes, drawing the egg mixture from the sides of the pan into the centre using a fork. Add the peas, sweetcorn and chopped tomatoes and continue cooking for 3–4 minutes until the eggs are set on the bottom. Put the pan under a preheated grill and cook for 2 minutes until the top of the frittata is lightly browned.

Sprinkle with the chopped parsley and cut into wedges. Serve with salad leaves and wholegrain bread.

CHEESE & SPINACH SOUFFLÉS

PREPARATION TIME 12–15 minutes

COOKING TIME 25–30 minutes

225 g baby spinach leaves

25 g sunflower margarine

25 g wholemeal flour

½ teaspoon mustard powder

150 ml milk

½ teaspoon freshly grated nutmeg

3 eggs, separated

50 g mature Cheddar cheese, grated, plus 2 teaspoons extra for sprinkling

freshly ground black pepper

a baking sheet

6 ramekins, 150 ml each, lightly greased

serves 6

Preheat the oven to 180°C (350°F) Gas 4 and put a baking sheet in to heat up 5 minutes before cooking.

Rinse the spinach, drain well, then put it in a saucepan with only the water clinging to the leaves. Cook over medium heat for 2–3 minutes until just wilted. Drain well, squeezing out any excess water, then chop it finely.

Put the margarine in a heavy based saucepan and melt over low heat. Using a wooden spoon, stir in the flour and mustard powder and cook, stirring constantly, for 2 minutes. Remove the pan from the heat and gradually stir in the milk. Return the pan to the heat and cook, stirring, until the sauce is thick and smooth. Remove the pan from the heat and let cool slightly before adding the nutmeg and black pepper to taste.

Add the egg yolks to the sauce one at a time, beating after each addition. Add the spinach, then stir in the cheese until melted.

Put the egg whites in a clean, grease-free bowl and whisk until stiff peaks form. Gradually stir them into the sauce, but don't overmix. Put the prepared ramekins on the preheated baking sheet and spoon the mixture into them, filling them about three-quarters full. Sprinkle the tops with the extra cheese and bake in the preheated oven for 20–25 minutes until well risen and golden brown. Serve immediately.

SIMPLE VEGETABLE QUICHE

Kids love quiche and this meat-free version is a great way to increase your child's vegetable intake. Almost any vegetables can be used, so be creative. The eggs provide an excellent source of protein, zinc, omega 3 fatty acids and vitamins A, D, E and B12.

PREPARATION TIME 15 minutes
COOKING TIME 1 hour

1 shop-bought wholemeal pastry case

filling

100 g broccoli, divided into small florets

1 tablespoon olive oil

1 onion, finely chopped

1 small red pepper, sliced into rings and deseeded

1 carrot, about 75 g, grated

3 eggs

150 ml semi-skimmed milk (use whole milk for children under 5)

¼ teaspoon freshly grated nutmeg

freshly ground black pepper

to serve (optional)

salad leaves

boiled new potatoes

a baking sheet

serves 6–8

Unwrap the pastry case and put it on a baking sheet.

Steam the broccoli florets over a saucepan of gently simmering water for 3 minutes. Plunge them into cold water and drain well.

Heat the oil in a non-stick frying pan, add the onion and fry gently for 5 minutes, stirring frequently. Transfer the onion to the pastry case, spreading it evenly over the base. Arrange the broccoli, pepper and carrot on top of the onion. Put the eggs, milk, nutmeg and black pepper in a bowl and beat well. Pour the mixture over the vegetables in the pastry case.

Bake in a preheated oven at 200°C (400°F) Gas 6 for 15 minutes. Reduce the temperature to 180°C (350°F) Gas 4 and continue to bake for about 20 minutes until the filling is set. Serve with salad and new potatoes, if liked.

COOK'S TIPS

- Ready-made wholemeal pastry cases are available from health food stores.
- The cooked quiches can be frozen for up to 1 month.
- If you have the time to make the pastry case yourself, make the pastry as directed on page 129, but omit the orange zest. Line a 23 cm diameter, loose-based tart tin with the rolled pastry. Put some crumpled foil in the case and bake it in a preheated oven at 200°C (400°F) Gas 6 for 15 minutes. Remove the foil and return the case to the oven for 5 minutes until set and lightly golden. Remove from the oven and let cool slightly. Continue as for the main recipe, above.

VARIATIONS

- Sprinkle the quiche with a little grated cheese just before baking.
- Add 1 tablespoon canned cannellini beans to the filling.
- Replace the broccoli and carrot with about 200 g finely chopped, well drained, blanched spinach and 75 g crumbled goats' cheese.

Did You Know?

According to recent government figures, the average British child eats fewer than half of the recommended five portions of fruit and vegetables a day, while almost 15 per cent of children between the ages of five and 15 eat none.

PIZZA

There are so many reasons to make this, I don't know where to begin. Unlike most shop-bought pizzas, which consist of cardboard-like bases made from highly refined white flour and toppings of the smallest amount of tomato paste and a scattering of ready grated processed cheese, your home-made version will be both healthy and delicious.

PREPARATION TIME 15–20 minutes, plus 1 hour rising time
COOKING TIME 12–15 minutes

500 g strong wholemeal bread flour

225 g strong white bread flour, plus extra for sprinkling and dusting

1 sachet (3 teaspoons) quick-acting yeast

1½ teaspoons salt

1 tablespoon light muscovado sugar

3 tablespoons olive oil

about 500 ml tepid water

1 quantity Tomato Sauce (page 86)

fresh herbs, such as basil or oregano, to serve

toppings, your choice of:
Vegetables: baby asparagus spears, sliced tomatoes, thinly sliced courgette, sliced peppers, sweetcorn kernels, peas, lightly steamed sugar snap peas or mangetout, onion rings fried in a little olive oil until softened, lightly steamed broccoli florets, blanched spinach, sliced mushrooms, pitted olives

Meat: strips of ham,; grilled bacon rashers, chopped; strips of prosciutto; shredded cooked chicken breast; slices of premium quality sausage

Fish: flaked canned tuna, smoked or canned mackerel, flaked smoked salmon

Cheese: mozzarella, Cheddar, Gouda, Gruyère, goats' cheese

2 baking sheets, lightly greased

makes 8

Sift the flours into a large mixing bowl, adding the bran left in the sieve, and stir in the yeast, salt and sugar. Make a well in the centre and pour in the olive oil then gradually add the tepid water, mixing the flour into the liquid. Add enough water to form a smooth and pliable dough.

Turn the dough out on to a lightly floured work surface and knead for 10 minutes or until smooth and elastic. Put the dough in a clean, oiled bowl (or in an oiled plastic bag), cover and let rise until doubled in size (about 1 hour).

Divide the dough into 8 equal balls and knead each one into a round. Roll each round on a lightly floured work surface to a circle about 16 cm diameter. Transfer the pizza bases to the baking sheets.

Spread each base with 2 tablespoons of the tomato sauce, then add your choice of topping. Kids love to help put these together.

Bake in a preheated oven at 230°C (450°F) Gas 8 for 12–15 minutes or until the bases are golden and the tops are bubbling. Sprinkle with fresh herbs, if using, and serve immediately.

COOK'S TIPS
• Any leftover dough can be wrapped and frozen for up to 1 month. Let the dough thaw thoroughly before shaping and using.
• Children love to 'build' their own pizzas, so why not put bowls of different ingredients on the kitchen table and let them help themselves? This can work really well on special occasions such as parties or weekend suppers. When arranging the ingredients on the pizza base, start with the larger ingredients, such as strips of pepper, asparagus or sliced tomato and finish with the smaller ingredients, such as sliced mushrooms and finally sprinkle with grated cheese.

VARIATION
• To make 8–10 mini party pizzas, use half the amount of dough given above (freeze the rest). Divide the dough into balls about the size of an egg. Roll out on a lightly floured work surface to form a circle about 8 cm diameter and 1 cm thick. Spread with a little of the prepared tomato sauce, then let the children build up their own pizzas from the prepared toppings. Bake as in the main recipe for 8–10 minutes.

BAKED SWEET POTATOES WITH CHEESY LENTIL HASH & CRISPY BACON

Sweet potatoes and lentils are low-glycaemic index foods, which means they release their sugars into the blood stream at a slow and steady rate, helping to keep children's energy levels constant. Lentils are also an excellent source of protein, iron, selenium and potassium – a mineral which helps to counteract the effects of too much salt in the diet.

PREPARATION TIME
12 minutes
COOKING TIME 45–50 minutes

4 medium sweet potatoes, about 100 g each

200 g red split lentils

450–500 ml vegetable stock

1–2 garlic cloves, crushed

1 onion, very finely chopped

2 celery stalks, very thinly sliced

1 tablespoon soy sauce

2 tablespoons tomato purée

6 rashers lean back bacon, grilled and chopped

100 g extra mature Cheddar cheese, grated

an ovenproof dish

serves 4

Lightly prick the sweet potatoes with a fork and bake directly on the shelves of a preheated oven at 200°C (400°F) Gas 6 for 35–40 minutes until soft when gently squeezed. Remove and leave until cool enough to handle.

Meanwhile, put the lentils in a saucepan, add the stock and bring to the boil. Cover, reduce the heat and simmer for 20–25 minutes until soft. Add more stock or water if the lentils start to dry out.

Meanwhile, put the garlic, onion, celery, soy sauce and 3–4 tablespoons water in a non-stick frying pan and heat gently for about 10 minutes or until the vegetables are soft. Add them to the saucepan of cooked lentils along with the tomato purée, chopped grilled bacon and half the grated cheese. Mix well, then reheat gently, stirring occasionally, until hot.

Cut the cooked sweet potatoes in half. Put them in an ovenproof dish and top with the lentil mixture. Sprinkle with the remaining cheese and cook under a preheated hot grill for 10 minutes or until the cheese is golden and bubbling. Serve hot.

COOK'S TIP

• To cook the sweet potatoes in a microwave, wrap them in kitchen paper and cook each one on HIGH for 4–4½ minutes. Let stand for 1 minute before topping with the lentils and grilling as in the main recipe, above. If you cook more than 1 potato at a time, increase the cooking time accordingly.

VARIATION

• Top the sweet potatoes with Home-made Baked Beans (page 76) instead of the lentils.

WARM POTATO SALAD

This versatile salad can be eaten hot or cold, as a meal in itself or as an accompaniment to burgers or grilled chicken.

PREPARATION TIME
15 minutes
COOKING TIME 15–20 minutes

450 g salad potatoes, such as Pink Fir or Charlotte, unpeeled

1 tablespoon natural yoghurt

1 tablespoon half fat crème fraîche

1 garlic clove, crushed

½ cucumber, finely chopped

1 small red pepper, deseeded and finely chopped

2 hard boiled eggs, chopped (page 41)

serves 4

Boil the potatoes in a large saucepan of simmering water for 15–20 minutes until the potatoes are tender when pierced with a fork. Drain and let cool slightly. When cool enough to handle, cut them into 2.5 cm cubes and put in a serving bowl.

Put the yoghurt, crème fraîche and garlic in a separate bowl and mix. Spoon the mixture over the potatoes, add the cucumber, pepper and eggs and stir carefully. Serve hot or cold.

WALNUT PESTO

Walnuts are an excellent source of omega 3 fatty acids, which are important for healthy brain development and can help reduce the risk of heart disease.

PREPARATION TIME
8–10 minutes

50 g walnut halves

50 g Parmesan cheese, grated

50 g fresh basil leaves

3 garlic cloves, crushed

90–100 ml extra virgin olive oil

400 g freshly cooked pasta,
to serve

serves 4

Put the walnuts in a food processor and grind to a fine meal. Add the cheese, basil and garlic and blend for 2 minutes. With the machine running, gradually add the oil through the feed tube and blend to a smooth, slightly grainy paste. Add more oil, if necessary. Spoon the pesto into a sterilized jar (page 4) and store, covered, in the refrigerator for up to 5 days.

To serve, stir into freshly cooked, hot pasta.

TOMATO SAUCE FOR PASTA

This sauce is so versatile that I suggest making four times the quantity here and freezing what you don't need immediately. It can also be used on Pizza (page 82) or poured over grilled chicken or fish.

PREPARATION TIME 5–8 minutes
COOKING TIME 22 minutes

1 tablespoon olive oil

1 small onion, finely chopped

2 garlic cloves, crushed

1 red pepper, deseeded and finely chopped

400 g canned chopped tomatoes

1–2 tablespoons tomato purée

1 teaspoon sugar

Worcestershire sauce, to taste (optional)

2 tablespoons chopped fresh basil leaves

sea salt and freshly ground black pepper

to serve

400 g freshly cooked pasta

freshly grated Parmesan cheese

serves 4; makes 600 ml

Heat the oil in a large, heavy based saucepan, add the onion, garlic and pepper and fry gently, stirring occasionally, for 8–10 minutes until softened but not browned. Add the tomatoes, tomato purée, sugar and 200 ml water. Bring to the boil, then reduce the heat and simmer gently for 10–12 minutes until reduced and thickened. Stir in the Worcestershire sauce, if using, basil and salt and pepper, to taste.

Spoon the sauce over freshly cooked, hot pasta and serve immediately, sprinkled with some freshly grated Parmesan cheese.

COOK'S TIPS
- If your children prefer a smoother sauce, transfer the sauce to a food processor or blender and blend briefly until smooth.
- Any leftover sauce can be poured into sterilized jars (page 4) and stored in the refrigerator for up to 1 week. Alternatively, pour the sauce into small, freezerproof containers and freeze for up to 2 months.

VARIATION
- To make a super-speedy ragù, you will need 300 g lean minced beef (use soya mince for vegetarians). Gently heat 1 tablespoon olive oil in a non-stick saucepan, add the mince and fry gently for 5 minutes until sealed, then cook for a further 15 minutes or until the mince is cooked, stirring frequently to break up any lumps. Add 300 ml of the prepared tomato sauce and heat through for about 5 minutes until piping hot. Serve with freshly cooked pasta.

TUSCAN TUNA & BEAN SAUCE

This is the fastest, easiest pasta sauce you can make and it's so filling it can almost be served as a meal in itself with some crusty wholemeal bread.

PREPARATION TIME 3–5 minutes
COOKING TIME 5 minutes

400 g canned chopped tomatoes

200 g canned tuna in spring water, drained

300 g canned beans, such as red kidney, butter bean or haricot, drained and rinsed

100 ml vegetable stock

1 tablespoon chopped fresh coriander

sea salt and freshly ground black pepper

500 g freshly cooked pasta, to serve

serves 6; makes 500 ml

Put the tomatoes, tuna, beans, stock, coriander, and salt and pepper in a food processor and blend until smooth. Pour the mixture into a saucepan and heat, stirring occasionally, for about 5 minutes until piping hot. Alternatively, pour the mixture into a microwaveable bowl, cover with microwaveable clingfilm, pierce it and heat on HIGH for 2 minutes. Stir and heat on HIGH for 1 minute more. Remove and let stand for 1 minute.

Spoon the sauce over freshly cooked, hot pasta, to serve.

COOK'S TIP

• For a chunkier sauce, simply put all the ingredients in a saucepan – there's no need to blend them. Stir well and heat gently until piping hot. Spoon over hot pasta, to serve.

ROASTED VEGETABLE SAUCE

I love this recipe because although there is a bit of work involved in chopping the vegetables, once they are prepared you simply pop them in the oven and forget about them for 40 minutes. You can serve the vegetables on their own, straight out of the oven, sprinkled with a little chopped ham and grated cheese.

PREPARATION TIME 12–15 minutes
COOKING TIME 35–45 minutes

1 sweet potato, cut into cubes

1 large carrot, sliced

1 onion, thickly sliced

2 courgettes, thickly sliced

1 red pepper, deseeded and chopped

1 yellow pepper, deseeded and chopped

2 celery stalks, sliced

12 cherry tomatoes, halved

4 garlic cloves, finely chopped

2 tablespoons olive oil

4 sprigs of fresh rosemary

400 g canned chopped tomatoes

sea salt and freshly ground black pepper

400 g freshly cooked pasta, to serve

serves 8; makes 1.25 litres

Put all the fresh vegetables and the garlic in a roasting tin and pour over the olive oil. Toss well to coat, then top with the rosemary sprigs. Roast in a preheated oven at 200°C (400°F) Gas 6 for 30–40 minutes, stirring occasionally, until the vegetables are soft.

Remove from the oven and discard the rosemary. Let cool slightly, then stir in the canned tomatoes. Transfer the vegetables to a food processor and blend, in batches if necessary, until smooth. Add a little water if the sauce is too thick.

Transfer to a saucepan, season to taste with salt and pepper, then reheat gently for about 5 minutes until hot.

Spoon the sauce over freshly cooked, hot pasta, to serve.

COOK'S TIP

• When cold, spoon the sauce into small freezerproof containers. Label them and freeze for up to 2 months. Stir well when reheating.

VARIATION

• The sauce can also be served on top of grilled meat, burgers (pages 106–109) or baked potatoes.

FISH FINGERS WITH SWEET POTATO CHIPS & PEA PUREE

Here is a really healthy alternative to the all-time favourite, fish fingers, chips and peas. The fish fingers are made from 100 per cent fresh fish coated in wholemeal breadcrumbs. The chips are replaced with vitamin- and fibre-packed sweet potatoes that are lightly baked in sunflower oil instead of being deep fried, while the Real Tomato Ketchup adds a healthy dose of disease-fighting vitamins without all that unnecessary sugar.

PREPARATION TIME 15 minutes, plus 30 minutes chilling time
COOKING TIME 25 minutes

4 fillets of white fish, such as cod, haddock or coley, about 100 g each, skinned

2–3 tablespoons wholemeal flour

1 egg, beaten

150 g fresh wholemeal breadcrumbs, made from at least 2-day-old bread

Real Tomato Ketchup (page 105), to serve

sweet potato chips

4 sweet potatoes, cut into wedges

2 tablespoons sunflower oil

pea purée

400 g frozen peas

1 tablespoon half fat crème fraîche

a baking sheet, lightly greased

serves 4–6

Remove any fine bones from the fish and cut each fillet into 5 strips. Take 3 shallow dishes, put the flour in one, the beaten egg in another and the breadcrumbs in the third. First, coat a fish strip in the flour, then dip it into the egg, shaking off any excess, then coat it in breadcrumbs. Transfer to a large plate. Repeat with the remaining fish strips until they are all coated. Lightly cover the coated fish with clingfilm and chill in the refrigerator for at least 30 minutes.

To make the sweet potato chips, bring a large saucepan of water to the boil and add the wedges. Return the water to the boil and cook for 3–5 minutes until the sweet potatoes have softened. Drain well and transfer to a roasting tin. Pour over the oil and toss gently to coat. Cook on the top shelf of a preheated oven at 200°C (400°F) Gas 6 for 15 minutes, turning the chips occasionally, until crisp and golden.

Meanwhile, put the fish fingers on the prepared baking sheet and cook on the middle shelf of the preheated oven for about 10 minutes until golden.

To make the pea purée, put the peas in a microwaveable jug and add 2 tablespoons water. Microwave on HIGH for 6 minutes, then let stand for 1 minute. Add the crème fraîche and blend roughly with a hand-held blender. Alternatively, cook the peas in a saucepan of boiling water for 3 minutes. Drain well, transfer to a blender or food processor, add the crème fraîche and blend to a purée.

Serve the fish fingers accompanied by the sweet potato chips and pea purée.

COOK'S TIP
- If you use fresh fish, you can freeze the coated fingers. Put them on a large, flat tray and open freeze until frozen, then pack in a freezerproof container, label, date and freeze for up to 1 month.

Did You Know?

Sweet potatoes contain vitamins A and C, they are a good source of fibre, which keeps the digestive tract healthy, and phytochemicals to protect against disease. They also release their sugars at a slower and steadier pace than regular potatoes helping to keep energy levels constant.

FISH CAKES

Even children who turn up their noses at fish will usually eat fish cakes. These are packed with quality fish and are completely additive-free.

PREPARATION TIME 15 minutes, plus 30 minutes chilling time
COOKING TIME 25 minutes

400 g potatoes, cut into large chunks

500 g white fish fillet such as cod loin or haddock

300 ml semi skimmed milk (use whole milk for children under 5)

a handful of fresh flat leaf parsley sprigs

1 bay leaf

1 tablespoon finely grated unwaxed lemon zest

2 tablespoons chopped fresh herbs, such as dill, parsley or coriander

2–3 tablespoons wholemeal flour

2–3 tablespoons sunflower oil

sea salt and freshly ground black pepper

lemony green beans

150 g green beans

1 tablespoon freshly squeezed lemon juice

1 tablespoon extra virgin olive oil

makes 8 small fish cakes

Cook the potatoes in a large saucepan of boiling water for 15 minutes until tender. Drain and mash.

Meanwhile, rinse the fish and put it in a frying pan with the milk, parsley sprigs and bay leaf. Bring to the boil, then cover and simmer for about 10 minutes until the fish is cooked and the flesh looks white. Remove the fish with a slotted spoon and transfer it to a large bowl. Let it cool slightly and when cool enough to handle, remove the skin and any bones and flake the flesh. Discard the cooking liquor.

Add the mashed potato, lemon zest and chopped herbs to the fish. Season to taste with salt and pepper, then mix lightly. Using your hands, shape the mixture into 8 small fish cakes. Put the flour on a plate and coat the fish cakes in it. Transfer the fish cakes to a plate, cover lightly with clingfilm and chill in the refrigerator for at least 30 minutes.

To make the lemony green beans, lightly steam the beans for about 5 minutes until cooked but still slightly crunchy. Drain well, transfer to a warmed serving bowl and add the lemon juice, olive oil and a sprinkling of salt. Toss well and cover to keep warm.

To cook the fish cakes, heat the sunflower oil in a frying pan. Add the fish cakes and cook for 4–5 minutes on each side until golden brown, crisp and piping hot. Serve immediately with the lemony green beans.

COOK'S TIPS
* Make double quantities of the fish cakes and freeze half of them after shaping. Ensure that you use fresh fish if freezing. Put them on a large, flat tray and open freeze until frozen, then pack in a freezerproof container, label, date and freeze for up to 1 month.
* The fish cakes can be grilled or oven-baked instead of pan-fried. Brush lightly with a little oil, then cook under a preheated moderate grill for 4–5 minutes on each side. Alternatively, put them on a baking sheet, brush lightly with oil and cook in a preheated oven at 190°C (375°F) Gas 5 for 15–18 minutes until golden brown and piping hot.

VARIATIONS
* Replace the cod or haddock with salmon fillet.
* Add some chopped, cooked peeled prawns, thawed if frozen.
* Serve the fish cakes with a little hot Roasted Vegetable Sauce (page 89) poured over the top.

FISH PIE

Protein, essential fatty acids, calcium, iron, fibre – you name it, this fish pie has got it. Every mouthful will help build fitter, stronger, healthier little bodies.

PREPARATION TIME 20 minutes
COOKING TIME 45–50 minutes

500 g potatoes, cut into large chunks

500 g cod or haddock fillet

400 ml semi-skimmed milk (use whole milk for children under 5)

1 bay leaf

250 g canned mackerel fillets in oil, drained

2 hard-boiled eggs, roughly chopped

200 g baby spinach leaves

150 g frozen peas

5 tablespoons sunflower oil

4 tablespoons plain flour

1 large leek, thinly sliced

50 g Cheddar cheese, grated (optional)

sea salt and freshly ground black pepper

honey glazed carrots (optional)

about 700 g baby carrots

4 teaspoons clear honey

1 tablespoon unsalted butter

8 ramekins or small ovenproof dishes, 150 ml each

serves 8

Cook the potatoes in a large saucepan of boiling water for 15 minutes until tender. Drain and mash.

Rinse the cod or haddock and put it in a frying pan. Add the milk and bay leaf and bring to the boil. Reduce the heat to a simmer and cook for 10 minutes. Remove the pan from the heat and strain off and reserve the cooking liquor. When the fish is cool enough to handle, remove the skin and any bones, then flake it. Flake the mackerel into small pieces and add it to the cooked fish, along with the chopped eggs.

Meanwhile, put the spinach and peas in a steamer placed over gently simmering water and cook for 3 minutes. Squeeze out any excess water from the spinach and chop it. Stir the spinach and peas into the fish mixture, then divide it between the 8 ramekins.

Make the reserved cooking liquor up to 400 ml, if necessary, with more milk or water. Heat 4 tablespoons oil in a small saucepan and stir in the flour. Cook over low heat, stirring continuously, for 2 minutes. Remove the pan from the heat and gradually stir in the reserved cooking liquor. Return the pan to the heat and cook, stirring continuously, until the sauce thickens. Season to taste with salt and pepper, then pour the sauce over the fish in the ramekins.

Heat the remaining oil in a frying pan. Add the sliced leek and cook for 5 minutes until softened. Divide the leeks between the ramekins, then top each one with the mashed potato. Sprinkle the tops with a little grated cheese, if using. Bake in a preheated oven at 190°C (375°F) Gas 5 for 20–25 minutes until golden brown and bubbling.

Meanwhile, to make the honey-glazed carrots, if using, put the carrots in a steamer placed over gently simmering water and cook for 10–12 minutes until tender when pierced with a fork. Transfer the carrots to a warm serving bowl. Pour over the honey, add the butter and stir until well coated.

Serve the fish pie immediately, accompanied by the warm carrots, if using.

COOK'S TIP
- To freeze the fish pies, assemble them, then let cool completely. Wrap well and freeze for up to 1 month. Remove the pies from the freezer the day before you want to cook them. Let them defrost thoroughly in the refrigerator, then pop them in the oven and cook as above.

CHICKEN & VEGETABLE FAJITAS

I don't know who loves this recipe the most in my family, the adults or the kids. It is full of fibre and foods that release their sugars at a steady pace into the blood stream – a great meal for ensuring your children's energy levels stay constant.

PREPARATION TIME 20 minutes
COOKING TIME 25 minutes

2 boneless, skinless chicken breasts, about 100 g each

1 tablespoon olive oil

1 yellow pepper, deseeded and sliced

1 green pepper, deseeded and sliced

400 g canned chopped tomatoes

1–2 garlic cloves, crushed

1 teaspoon mild chilli powder (optional)

¼ teaspoon dried oregano

1 tablespoon tomato purée

400 g canned refried beans; or borlotti or pinto beans, rinsed, drained and mashed

4 large wheat tortillas, 20 cm diameter

50–100 g extra mature Cheddar cheese

2 tablespoons half fat crème fraîche

2 tablespoons chopped fresh coriander

salsa

2 ripe, but still firm tomatoes, about 175 g, halved, deseeded and finely chopped

1 garlic clove, crushed

2 spring onions, finely chopped (optional)

1–2 teaspoons freshly squeezed lemon juice

1 tablespoon chopped fresh coriander

serves 4

To make the salsa, put the tomatoes, garlic, spring onions, if using, lemon juice and coriander in a bowl. Stir well. Spoon into a small dish, cover and set aside for 30 minutes for the flavours to develop. (If not using immediately, cover tightly with non-pvc cling wrap and store in the refrigerator for up to 3 days. Stir before use.)

Rinse the chicken breasts and pat dry with kitchen paper. Heat a stove-top grill pan until smoking. Add the chicken to the pan and cook for 8–9 minutes on each side until thoroughly cooked. To check, pierce the thickest part with a skewer; the juices should run clear. If there is any sign of blood, continue to cook for a few minutes more. Remove the chicken from the pan and slice it thinly.

Heat the oil in a saucepan, add the peppers and fry gently for 10 minutes until soft. Stir in the tomatoes, garlic, chilli powder, if using, oregano and tomato purée. Bring to the boil, reduce the heat and simmer for about 10 minutes until the mixture has reduced slightly and thickened.

Put the beans in a small, heavy based saucepan and heat gently, stirring frequently, until smooth and piping hot.

Wrap the tortillas in foil and heat in a preheated oven at 200°C (400°F) Gas 6 for 6–7 minutes until soft and piping hot. Alternatively, heat in a microwave oven according to the directions on the packet.

Spread each tortilla with a thick layer of mashed beans, 1–2 tablespoons of the tomato and pepper mixture and one-quarter of the chicken slices. Sprinkle with grated cheese, salsa, crème fraîche and coriander. Roll up and serve immediately.

VARIATION

- For a vegetarian alternative, omit the chicken breast and replace it with some sliced ripe avocado and cucumber.

Did You Know?

Tomatoes are an excellent source of lycopene, a powerful antioxidant that helps to protect against cancer and heart disease. The body can absorb lycopene easier if the tomatoes are cooked rather than raw and if there is a little bit of oil present, so this recipe is perfect!

CHICKEN & PEA RISOTTO

Adults and children alike will love this protein-packed risotto. Skinless chicken contains very little fat and peas are a great source of immune-boosting vitamins A and C, as well as B vitamins – necessary for the development of a healthy nervous system and essential for growth – and folic acid.

PREPARATION TIME 10–12 minutes
COOKING TIME 30–35 minutes

850–900 ml hot chicken stock

1 tablespoon sunflower oil

1 onion, finely chopped

2 garlic cloves, crushed

2 celery stalks, chopped

250 g boneless, skinless chicken breast, cut into bite-sized cubes

200 g risotto rice, such as arborio

100 g courgettes, grated

200 g frozen peas

2 tablespoons half fat crème fraîche

freshly ground black pepper

1 tablespoon chopped fresh flat leaf parsley, to serve

serves 4–6

Put the stock in a saucepan and keep it at a gentle simmer.

Heat the oil in a large, heavy based saucepan and add the onion, garlic and celery. Cook gently for 5 minutes until softened and translucent but not browned. Add the chicken and cook for another 5 minutes, stirring frequently, until the chicken is sealed. Stir in the rice and cook for 1–2 minutes until the rice smells toasted and looks opaque.

Begin adding the stock, a large ladle at a time, stirring gently until each ladle has been absorbed by the rice. The rice should always be at a gentle simmer. Continue in this way for 10 minutes, then add the courgettes and peas to the pan. Continue adding stock as before until the rice is tender and creamy but the grains still firm, this should take a further 5–10 minutes.

Taste and season with pepper, then stir in the crème fraîche. Cover and let rest for a few minutes. Serve sprinkled with chopped parsley.

VARIATION
• Use ham or smoked haddock fillet instead of the chicken.

Did You Know?
Frozen vegetables usually contain just as many vitamins and minerals as fresh ones. They are great for busy parents because they require no preparation and can be on the table in minutes.

READY, STEADY, GO STIR FRY

Lots of parents rule out stir fry when it comes to feeding their children, but in my experience children really like it, if they are given a chance to taste it. The key is to make sure the vegetables retain some crunch (there's nothing kids hate more than soggy vegetables) and to cut the chicken into manageable strips.

PREPARATION TIME 15 minutes
COOKING TIME 12 minutes

2 garlic cloves, crushed

1 tablespoon sesame seeds

1–2 tablespoons soy sauce

2 teaspoons clear honey

2 boneless, skinless chicken breasts, about 100 g each

2 tablespoons groundnut or sunflower oil

1 red pepper, deseeded and thinly sliced

1 yellow pepper, deseeded and thinly sliced

1 green pepper, deseeded and thinly sliced

100 g mini sweetcorn

50 g mangetout

225 g fine egg noodles

serves 4

Put the garlic, sesame seeds, soy sauce, honey and 2 tablespoons water in a small bowl and mix well.

Cut the chicken into thin slices. Heat a wok until hot. Add the oil and heat until hot. Carefully add the chicken to the wok and stir fry for 3 minutes, stirring frequently, until the chicken is sealed. Add the peppers and fry for 3 minutes, stirring frequently. Add the sweetcorn and mangetout and fry for 2 minutes more.

Meanwhile, put the noodles in a saucepan of gently simmering water. Remove the pan from the heat and set aside for 3 minutes to let the noodles soften.

Add the soy sauce mixture to the wok, stir well and cook for 2–3 minutes until the chicken is thoroughly cooked, but the vegetables still retain some bite.

Drain the noodles, divide them between 4 warmed bowls, top with the stir fry mixture and serve immediately.

COOK'S TIPS
- It is important that the wok is preheated before adding the oil. This helps to prevent the chicken sticking to it and ensures that the chicken cooks quickly.
- Groundnut or sunflower oil is better for stir frying than olive oil.

VARIATIONS
- Use strips of turkey or beef fillet instead of the chicken.
- Fish can also be used – try large peeled prawns or strips of monkfish.
- Try other vegetables, such as asparagus, sugar snap peas, sliced courgettes and sliced carrots or broccoli florets.

Did You Know?
The colour of a fruit or vegetable is often a good indication of its nutrient content. Green foods are often rich in the antioxidant vitamins A, C and E. Red ones contain lycopene, a powerful cancer-fighting carotenoid, while immune-boosting beta-carotene is found in orange and yellow foods.

CHICKEN NUGGETS WITH OVEN-BAKED WEDGES

Unlike the shop-bought varieties, these chicken nuggets contain 100 per cent lean meat, so they are high in protein and low in fat. The potato wedges are also very low in fat as they are baked in the oven instead of being deep fried.

PREPARATION TIME 15 minutes
COOKING TIME 30 minutes

100 g wholemeal flour or wheatgerm

1 garlic clove, crushed

25 g finely grated mature Cheddar or Parmesan cheese

90 ml water

1 egg white

3 boneless, skinless chicken breasts, about 100 g each, cut into bite-sized pieces

sea salt and freshly ground black pepper

Real Tomato Ketchup (page 105), to serve

oven-baked wedges

2 baking potatoes, about 350 g in total, cut into wedges

2 tablespoons sunflower oil

a baking sheet, lightly greased

serves 4

To make the potato wedges, bring a large saucepan of water to the boil and add the potato pieces. Cook for 10–12 minutes until slightly softened but still firm. Drain well and, when cool enough to handle, dry with kitchen paper. Transfer the wedges to a roasting tin and drizzle with the oil. Toss carefully so the potatoes are well coated. Sprinkle with a little sea salt. Cook on the top shelf of a preheated oven at 200°C (400°F) Gas 6 for about 15 minutes, stirring once, until golden brown and crisp.

Meanwhile, put the flour or wheatgerm, ½ teaspoon salt, garlic, cheese and black pepper, to taste, in a shallow dish. Put the water and egg white in a separate bowl and whisk lightly. Dip the chicken pieces in the egg white, then roll them in the flour or wheatgerm mixture until well coated. Transfer to the prepared baking sheet.

Put the baking sheet on the middle shelf of the preheated oven and cook at the same time as the potato wedges for 10–12 minutes, stirring occasionally, until the nuggets are thoroughly cooked.

Serve the nuggets with the oven-baked wedges and some real tomato ketchup.

Did You Know?

Chicken contains all the amino acids that growing bodies need. It also contains vitamin B12, which is needed for the formation of blood and nerve cells.

HOME-MADE SAUSAGES

Children love sausages. However, most versions often contain poor-quality meat as well as cheap fillers, additives and lots of salt. This recipe uses 100 per cent lean meat and adds flavour in the form of onion, garlic, apples and herbs.

PREPARATION TIME
15 minutes, plus 30 minutes chilling time
COOKING TIME 15–20 minutes

175 g cooking apples, peeled, cored and grated

300 g lean pork, such as loin, finely minced

1 medium onion, finely chopped

1–2 garlic cloves, crushed

2 tablespoons chopped fresh sage leaves

4 tablespoons wholemeal flour

2 tablespoons sunflower oil

sea salt and freshly ground black pepper

to serve
lightly steamed seasonal vegetables (optional)

Real Tomato Ketchup (see right)

makes 12

Wrap the grated apple tightly in a clean tea towel in order to remove some of the moisture. Put the apple, pork, onion, garlic and sage in a food processor. Add salt and pepper, to taste, then blend using the pulse button until mixed.

Transfer the mixture to a lightly floured work surface. Using damp hands, make 12 small balls about the size of a large apricot. Roll each one into a sausage shape. Put the flour in a shallow dish and coat the sausages evenly with it. Transfer the sausages to a large plate, cover lightly with clingfilm and chill in the refrigerator for 30 minutes.

Put the sausages in a non-stick roasting tin and drizzle with a little oil. Cook in a preheated oven at 190°C (375°F) Gas 5 for 15–20 minutes, turning them halfway through. Alternatively, heat the oil in a non-stick frying pan, add the sausages and cook for 12–15 minutes over moderate heat, turning frequently, until golden and thoroughly cooked.

Serve with lightly steamed seasonal vegetables, if liked, and real tomato ketchup.

VARIATIONS

- To serve, split a warmed pita bread and add a sausage, some shredded lettuce and a few tomato slices.
- Freshly ground lean beef steak or lamb can be used instead of the pork.
- Vary the flavours of the sausages by adding 2 tablespoons chopped fresh mixed herbs, 2–3 teaspoons mustard or horseradish or 25 g finely grated mature Cheddar cheese.

REAL TOMATO KETCHUP

PREPARATION TIME 15 minutes
COOKING TIME 2 hours

3 tablespoons olive oil

500 g onions, roughly chopped

3 garlic cloves, crushed

1.5 kg ripe tomatoes, roughly chopped

150 ml white wine vinegar

85–100 g dark muscovado sugar

½ teaspoon ground cloves

½ teaspoon ground allspice

1 teaspoon mustard seeds

½ teaspoon ground celery seeds

1 teaspoon sea salt

1 teaspoon freshly ground black pepper

makes 1.2 litres

Heat the oil in large, heavy based saucepan or preserving pan. Add the onions and cook for 8–10 minutes, stirring occasionally, until golden brown. Add the garlic and cook for 1 minute. Stir in the tomatoes, vinegar, sugar, cloves, allspice, mustard and celery seeds, and salt and pepper. Bring the mixture to the boil, cover, reduce the heat and simmer, stirring occasionally, for 1 hour.

Transfer the mixture to a blender or food processor and blend, in batches if necessary, to a fairly smooth purée. Return the purée to the rinsed pan and bring it to the boil. Reduce the heat, cover and simmer for about 45 minutes, stirring occasionally, until the mixture is thick. Remove the pan from the heat and let cool.

Once cool, pour the tomato sauce into small sterilized jars (page 4) and seal tightly. Store in the refrigerator for up to 1 month. Once opened, use within 1 week.

BURGERS

All kids love burgers. As you can see from these recipes, there is no reason why they should be unhealthy. In fact, they can be a great way of packaging up some really nutritious ingredients. Don't forget to make extra quantities for freezing.

CHICKEN BURGERS

PREPARATION TIME
20 minutes, plus 30 minutes chilling time
COOKING TIME 12–15 minutes

2 tablespoons olive oil

1 onion, finely chopped

1 celery stick, finely chopped

1 garlic clove, crushed

2 boneless, skinless chicken breasts, about 150 g in total, minced

100 g carrot, grated

1 tablespoon finely grated unwaxed orange zest

1–2 tablespoons chopped fresh parsley

50 g sultanas or dried cranberries

1 egg, beaten

2–3 tablespoons wholemeal flour, for coating

sea salt and freshly ground black pepper

to serve

4 wholemeal bread rolls

salad leaves

4 tomato slices

Real Tomato Ketchup (page 105)

serves 4

Heat the oil in a frying pan, add the onion, celery and garlic and fry for 5 minutes until soft. Transfer the mixture to a large bowl and add the chicken, carrot, orange zest, parsley, sultanas or cranberries and egg. Season to taste with salt and pepper and mix well.

Using damp hands, shape the mixture into 4 burgers. Put the flour in a shallow dish and evenly coat the burgers with it. Transfer them to a plate, cover lightly with clingfilm and chill in the refrigerator for 30 minutes.

Heat a non-stick frying pan, add the burgers and dry fry over medium heat for 5–6 minutes until golden underneath, then turn the burgers over and cook for 5–6 minutes on the other side until golden and thoroughly cooked.

To serve, put a burger in a wholemeal bread roll, top with crisp salad leaves, a slice of tomato and a little home-made tomato ketchup.

COOK'S TIP
- After being shaped, the burgers can be wrapped and frozen for up to 1 month.

BEEF BURGERS

PREPARATION TIME 8–10 minutes, plus 30 minutes chilling time
COOKING TIME 15–20 minutes

350 g extra lean beef steak, minced

1 small onion, finely chopped

50 g courgettes, grated

1 tablespoon chopped fresh flat leaf parsley or fresh sage leaves

freshly ground black pepper

lightly steamed seasonal vegetables, to serve

a baking sheet, lightly greased

makes 8

Put all the ingredients in a large bowl and mix with your hands until they come together to form a large ball. Shape the mixture into 8 balls and flatten them into burgers. Transfer to a large plate, lightly cover with clingfilm and chill in the refrigerator for 30 minutes.

Put the burgers on the prepared baking sheet and cook in a preheated oven at 190°C (375°F) Gas 5 for 15–20 minutes until thoroughly cooked. Alternatively, cook under a preheated hot grill for 4–6 minutes on each side, or dry fry in a hot, non-stick frying pan for 3–4 minutes on each side.

Serve with your choice of steamed vegetables.

COOK'S TIP
- After being shaped, the burgers can be wrapped and frozen for up to 1 month.

NUT BURGERS

PREPARATION TIME
20 minutes, plus 30 minutes
chilling time
COOKING TIME 30 minutes

225 g mixed unsalted nuts, such
as cashews, walnuts and peanuts

2 tablespoons olive oil

1 onion, very finely chopped

2 garlic cloves, crushed

75 g button mushrooms,
finely chopped

1 small yellow pepper, deseeded
and finely chopped

100 g fresh wholemeal
breadcrumbs

100 g carrot, grated

1 tablespoon chopped
fresh parsley

2–3 fresh sage leaves,
finely chopped

1 egg, beaten

wholemeal flour, for coating

sea salt and freshly ground
black pepper

to serve

4 wholemeal bread rolls

salad leaves

4 tomato slices

Real Tomato Ketchup (page 105)

a baking sheet, lightly greased

serves 4–6

Put the nuts in a food processor and blend until finely chopped.

Heat 1 tablespoon of the oil in a heavy based saucepan, add the onion and garlic and fry gently, stirring occasionally, for 5 minutes or until soft and golden. Add the mushrooms and pepper and cook for 3 minutes more. Remove the pan from the heat and mix in all the remaining ingredients except the flour and the remaining oil.

Using your hands, bring the mixture together to form a large ball, adding a little water if the mixture is too dry. Shape the mixture into 4 burgers. Put the flour in a shallow dish and coat the burgers evenly with it. Transfer to a plate, lightly cover with clingfilm and chill in the refrigerator for 30 minutes.

Put the burgers on the prepared baking sheet and brush lightly with the remaining oil. Bake in a preheated oven at 190°C (375°F) Gas 5 for 20 minutes until golden and piping hot. To serve, put a burger in a wholemeal bread roll, top with crisp salad leaves, a slice of tomato and a little home-made tomato ketchup.

VEGETABLE BURGERS

PREPARATION TIME 20 minutes,
plus 30 minutes chilling time
COOKING TIME 25–30 minutes

2–3 tablespoons sunflower oil

1 red onion, finely chopped

2 garlic cloves, crushed

100 g mushrooms, finely chopped

100 g unsalted cashew nuts, finely chopped

100 g cooked brown rice

150 g carrots, grated

50 g cooked peas

50 g cooked sweetcorn kernels

50 g fresh wholemeal breadcrumbs

5–6 tablespoons wholemeal flour

1 tablespoon chopped fresh parsley

sea salt and freshly ground black pepper

a baking sheet, lightly greased

serves 6

Heat 1 tablespoon of the oil in a saucepan. Add the onion and garlic and fry gently, stirring occasionally, for 5 minutes or until soft. Add the mushrooms and continue to cook, stirring occasionally, for 5 minutes until the vegetables are lightly cooked and golden.

Remove the pan from the heat and stir in the nuts, rice, carrots, peas, sweetcorn, breadcrumbs, 1–2 tablespoons flour, parsley and salt and pepper, to taste. Using damp hands, shape the mixture into 6 burgers. Coat them evenly in the remaining flour, then transfer to a plate, lightly cover with clingfilm and chill in the refrigerator for 30 minutes.

Put the burgers on the prepared baking sheet and brush lightly with the remaining oil. Bake in a preheated oven at 180°C (350°F) Gas 4 for 15–20 minutes until crisp and piping hot. Alternatively, cook under a preheated hot grill for 10–12 minutes, turning the burgers halfway through. Serve immediately.

MINI SHEPHERD'S PIES WITH FOUR VEG MASH

This recipe takes a little longer than most of the others to make, but you will have 8 mini pies that can be popped in the freezer and pulled out on those days when you don't have time to cook. There are 11 different vegetables in this dish – a real health booster.

PREPARATION TIME 25–30 minutes
COOKING TIME 45 minutes

1 tablespoon olive oil

200 g leeks, thinly sliced

600 g extra lean lamb mince

2 medium onions, finely chopped

2 celery sticks, finely chopped

1½ tablespoons wholemeal flour

½ tablespoon Worcestershire sauce

250 ml vegetable stock

225 g ripe tomatoes, chopped

1 red pepper, deseeded and chopped

2 carrots, grated

200 g frozen peas

75 g Cheddar cheese, grated

vegetable mash

175 g potatoes, chopped into small chunks

250 g sweet potatoes, chopped into small chunks

150 g carrots, chopped into small chunks

175 g parsnips, chopped into small chunks

freshly grated nutmeg, to taste

1–2 tablespoons milk or half fat crème fraîche

sea salt and freshly ground black pepper

8 individual ovenproof dishes, 350 ml each

makes 8 small pies

To make the vegetable mash, bring a large saucepan of water to the boil, add the potatoes, sweet potatoes, carrots and parsnips and cook for about 15 minutes until the vegetables are soft. Drain, return to the pan and mash. Add nutmeg, salt and pepper to taste and sufficient milk or crème fraîche to give a soft but not runny mixture. Set aside.

Heat the oil in a non-stick frying pan, add the leeks and fry gently for 5–8 minutes until soft. Remove the leeks with a slotted spoon and set aside.

Wipe the frying pan with kitchen paper, then return it to the heat. Add the lamb mince and dry fry for 5–8 minutes, stirring frequently, until sealed. Add the onions and celery and fry for a further 5 minutes. Drain through a colander to remove any fat, then return to the rinsed frying pan. Sprinkle in the flour and the Worcestershire sauce and cook, stirring, for 2 minutes. Slowly stir in the stock, tomatoes, pepper, carrots and peas. Bring to the boil, reduce the heat and simmer for 10–15 minutes until most of the excess liquid has been absorbed and the sauce is thick.

Spoon the meat mixture into the ovenproof dishes and top with a layer of the leeks. Spoon over the vegetable mash to cover the filling, then sprinkle with the grated cheese.

Cook under a preheated grill for 10–15 minutes until the tops are golden brown and bubbling. Alternatively, cook in a preheated oven at 190°C (375°F) Gas 5 for 20–25 minutes. Serve hot.

COOK'S TIP

- To freeze, prepare the pies and let cool completely. Wrap and label, then freeze for up to 1 month. Defrost thoroughly, then cook in a preheated oven at 190°C (375°F) Gas 5 for 20–25 minutes until piping hot.

VEGETABLES

It's a myth that kids won't eat vegetables. Dip asparagus spears in hot, melted garlic butter, add some chopped dry-cured bacon to peas or drizzle a little honey over baby carrots and watch those vegetables disappear! Here are a few more ideas.

BROCCOLI CHEESE

PREPARATION TIME 15–20 minutes
COOKING TIME 18–25 minutes

500 g broccoli, divided into bite-sized florets

cheese sauce

4 tablespoons sunflower oil

4 tablespoons plain flour

400 ml semi-skimmed milk (use whole milk for children under 5)

75 g mature Cheddar cheese grated, plus extra for sprinkling

an ovenproof dish

serves 4

Steam the broccoli over gently simmering water for 8 minutes or until it is tender but still has some bite. Drain and transfer to an ovenproof dish.

To make the cheese sauce, heat the oil in a small saucepan and stir in the flour. Cook, stirring, for 2 minutes. Remove the pan from the heat and gradually stir in the milk. Return the pan to the heat and cook, stirring continuously, until the sauce thickens.

Add the grated cheese to the sauce and stir until it has melted. Pour the sauce over the broccoli and sprinkle with a little more grated cheese. Cook under a preheated moderate grill for 10–15 minutes until the cheese is golden brown and bubbling. Serve.

SESAME SUGAR SNAP PEAS

PREPARATION TIME 4 minutes
COOKING TIME 4–5 minutes

1 tablespoon sunflower oil

400 g sugar snap peas

2 teaspoons sesame seeds

2 teaspoons sesame oil

serves 4

Heat a wok until hot, then add the sunflower oil. When the oil is hot, add the sugar snap peas. Stir fry for about 4 minutes, stirring continuously, until tender. Add the sesame seeds and oil and stir fry for 1 minute more. Serve immediately.

CREAMY SPINACH

PREPARATION TIME 5 minutes
COOKING TIME 3–4 minutes

500 g fresh spinach

2 tablespoons half fat crème fraîche

freshly grated nutmeg (optional)

serves 4

Discard any hard central stalks from the spinach and wash the leaves thoroughly in plenty of cold water. Drain well, then put the spinach in a large saucepan with only the water left clinging to the leaves. Cook for 2–3 minutes until wilted. Drain well, squeezing out any excess water. Chop finely.

Return the spinach to the rinsed pan and add 1 teaspoon water and the crème fraîche. Heat over medium heat for 1 minute, stirring. Serve immediately, sprinkled with a little freshly grated nutmeg, if using.

SHREDDED SPRING CABBAGE & HAM

PREPARATION TIME 5 minutes
COOKING TIME 6–7 minutes

500 g cabbage, such as Primo or spring

2 tablespoons half fat crème fraîche

2 thick slices of honey roasted ham, fat discarded, roughly chopped into small pieces

sea salt and freshly ground black pepper

serves 4

Remove any tough outer leaves and the hard central core from the cabbage and shred. Add the cabbage to a large saucepan of boiling water and return to the boil. Cover the pan, reduce the heat and simmer gently for 4–5 minutes until tender. Drain well.

Return the cabbage to the warm pan and stir in the crème fraîche, ham and salt and pepper, to taste. Heat gently, stirring, for 2 minutes until hot. Serve immediately.

PUDDINGS

Puddings offer a great opportunity to encourage children to eat more fruit. However, they can also fill them with lots of sugar, fat and additives they don't need. The nutritional content of some of the popular, commercially prepared puddings doesn't make happy reading.

CUSTARD Made in the traditional way – with eggs, milk and sugar – custard is a great source of protein, calcium, vitamins and minerals. However, many commercial varieties contain large amounts of sugar and additives, and some 'just-add-water' powdered versions even manage to bypass any nutritional benefits that may be had from adding fresh milk.

JELLY is a highly synthetic pudding consisting of little more than sugar, artificial colourings and flavourings and generous amounts of gelatin.

ICE CREAM As is often the case, the more expensive varieties tend to contain better quality ingredients. However, most shop-bought ice cream is a world away from the traditional recipe of milk, cream, sugar and eggs (page 117). Most contain a lot of fat and sugar and are bulked out with air and water. Production costs are kept to a minimum by using artificial colourings and flavourings, milk powders, emulsifiers and hardened vegetable fats.

MOUSSES Supermarkets now stock a vast array of mousse-like puddings. Most are little more than a blend of synthetic ingredients, such as emulsifiers, artificial colourings, flavourings and preservatives, and large amounts of sugar. The 'fruit' varieties contain very little, if any, fruit and most offer few or no nutritional benefits.

YOGHURT Plain yoghurt is a naturally healthy food that can be a good source of calcium, protein and vitamins. Those that are flavoured with natural fruit purées are also great choices. However, the potential health benefits of many yoghurts, especially those marketed specifically at children, are often outweighed by the high quantities of added sugar (some small pots contain as much as 4 teaspoons) or sweeteners, flavourings and additives. Many cheaper yoghurts contain no fruit at all, only chemical fruit flavours. Those that do contain fruit invariably contain artificial preservatives, too.

SERVING PUDDING

Children don't need pudding every day. It's far better to encourage them to get into the habit of heading for the fruit bowl if they want something sweet after dinner. Not serving puddings every day also helps to avoid the common scenario of the main meal being pushed aside in anticipation of something sweeter to come. Avoid the temptation to use puddings as a bribe to get your children to eat their main course. This will only serve to reinforce in their mind that savoury foods are to be endured and make sweet, fatty foods even more irresistible.

However, if you do serve a pudding, steer clear of commercially prepared ones as much as possible. In this chapter you'll find lots of fruit-packed ideas that are totally additive free and contain only the necessary amounts of sugar and fat. If you buy a ready-made pudding, check the label for the sugar content per 100 g: more than 10 g is high, less than 2 g is low.

REAL ALTERNATIVES
sprinkle bite-sized chunks of melon with a little grated nutmeg • cut a banana in half lengthways, put some chopped chocolate in the middle and heat for a few seconds in the microwave until the chocolate has melted • fresh fruit salad served with some half fat crème fraîche or Home-made Custard (page 126) • sliced mango served with fresh raspberries • fresh or frozen strawberries blended with Home-made Custard (page 126) • frozen summer fruits blended with low fat natural fromage frais and a little honey • fruit kebabs, grilled and drizzled with a little honey • Greek or natural yoghurt sweetened with honey and sprinkled with some Granola (page 32), finely chopped nuts or seeds to add extra crunch • fruit compote, either commercially prepared with no added sugar or home-made (page 121), topped with Granola (page 32) and a small scoop of home-made Vanilla Ice Cream (page 117) • chunks of low fat Cheddar cheese and apple on cocktail sticks • blend together a banana with some Home-made Custard (page 126), add 1 dessertspoon of grated chocolate (at least 70 per cent cocoa solids) and heat in the microwave on HIGH for 1 minute until the chocolate has melted

VANILLA ICE CREAM

All kids love ice cream. However, all but the most expensive shop-bought versions are little more than a cheap blend of artificial colourings and flavourings, milk powders, emulsifiers, sugars and hardened vegetable fats. This recipe is made in the old-fashioned way, using nothing but eggs, milk, sugar and cream. If you follow the variations, you can pack in a whole load of fruit too!

PREPARATION TIME 25 minutes
COOKING TIME 12–15 minutes
FREEZING TIME 3 hours

1 recipe Home-made Custard (page 126)

300 ml double cream

caster sugar, to taste

an ice cream maker (optional)

serves 6–8

Set the freezer to rapid freeze, or if using an ice cream maker, put the bowl in the freezer the night before.

Make the custard, cover with a piece of damp greaseproof paper and let cool. Whip the cream until soft peaks form, then stir it into the cooled custard. Taste and add a little caster sugar, if necessary.

Pour the mixture into a freezerproof container and freeze for 1 hour. Remove from the freezer and stir, breaking up any ice crystals that have formed. Return it to the freezer for a further 2 hours, stirring at least twice. Leave for a further 1 hour or until frozen.

If using an ice cream maker, pour the mixture into the machine and churn for 35–45 minutes or until softly frozen. Transfer to a freezerproof container, cover and label.

When ready to serve, transfer the ice cream to the refrigerator for at least 30 minutes to soften slightly. Serve in scoops.

The ice cream can be stored in the freezer for up to 1 month.

VARIATIONS

- **Fruit Ice Cream** Simmer 300 g ripe fruit (such as mango, raspberries, strawberries, papaya or mixed summer berries) with 4 tablespoons water and 1–2 tablespoons caster sugar for 5 minutes or until the fruit has collapsed. Let cool, transfer to a blender and process to a purée. Add the purée to the creamy custard mixture and continue as in the main recipe. Crushed ripe fruit can be added as well for added flavour.
- **Raspberry Ripple Ice Cream** Stir 150 ml raspberry purée (prepare as directed in Fruit Ice Cream, above) through the semi-frozen vanilla ice cream, giving a rippled effect. Do not stir the ice cream again after adding the purée.
- **Chocolate Ice Cream** Put 75 g finely chopped plain chocolate (at least 70 per cent cocoa solids) in a large heatproof bowl. Pour the hot custard onto the chocolate and stir until smooth. Cover and let cool, then continue as in the main recipe, above.
- Other ingredients can be folded into the ice cream before it is frozen. Try adding chopped nuts, chopped chocolate or chopped dried fruit, such as raisins, sultanas, apricots or cherries.

STICKY TOFFEE & APRICOT SAUCE

PREPARATION TIME 5–8 minutes
COOKING TIME 15–18 minutes

175 g ready-to-eat dried apricots, roughly chopped

25 g light muscovado sugar

15 g butter

makes 300 ml

Put the apricots, sugar and 200 ml water in a heavy based saucepan. Bring to the boil, then cover and reduce the heat. Simmer for 12–15 minutes or until the apricots are really soft. Let cool, then transfer to a blender and process to form a purée. Return the purée to the rinsed pan, add the butter and heat gently until the butter has melted. Stir, then serve poured over ice cream.

STRAWBERRY SAUCE

PREPARATION TIME 5–8 minutes
COOKING TIME 10 minutes

450 g strawberries, hulled

25–50 g caster sugar (depending on the ripeness of the strawberries)

2 tablespoons freshly squeezed lemon juice

makes 500 ml

Cut any large strawberries in half, then put them in a heavy based saucepan. Add the sugar, to taste, lemon juice and 150 ml water. Heat gently, stirring occasionally, until the sugar has dissolved.

Bring to the boil, reduce the heat and simmer for 5 minutes or until the strawberries are really soft.

Transfer to a blender and process to form a smooth sauce. Pour over ice cream, to serve.

VARIATION
• Other berries can be used in place of the strawberries. Try raspberries, blackberries, blueberries or a mixture. Plums, greengages or ripe mangoes can also be used.

KNICKERBOCKER GLORY

No childhood would be complete without the experience of eating a knickerbocker glory. These are packed full of fruit and made from home-made, additive-free ice cream, which is rich in both calcium and vitamin C.

PREPARATION TIME
10–15 minutes

500 g raspberries

½ recipe Chocolate Ice Cream (page 117)

300 ml natural yoghurt

225 g strawberries, halved if large

½ recipe Vanilla Ice Cream (page 117)

50 g plain chocolate (at least 70 per cent cocoa solids), roughly chopped or grated

4 tall sundae glasses

serves 4

Put 1 tablespoon raspberries in the bottom of each glass and top with 1 scoop of chocolate ice cream. Spoon over the yoghurt, then top with the strawberries, reserving 4 of the strawberries, to decorate.

Add 1 scoop of vanilla ice cream, then scatter over a little chopped chocolate. Add 1 more tablespoon of raspberries to each glass, then finish with 1 scoop of vanilla or chocolate ice cream. Sprinkle with a little more chopped chocolate, top with a strawberry and serve immediately.

Did You Know?
Strawberries contain more vitamin C than any other berry. Just one-quarter of the strawberries used here provides more than twice the amount a child needs in a day.

FRUIT COMPOTES

Stirred into yoghurt, ice cream and custard, blended into smoothies or eaten just as they are, fruit compotes are extremely versatile. Make double the quantity and freeze what you don't want to use immediately in small plastic containers. The compote can then be defrosted in the microwave at a moment's notice.

RHUBARB COMPOTE

PREPARATION TIME
5–8 minutes
COOKING TIME 15 minutes

2 tablespoons ginger ale

50 g caster sugar

450 g rhubarb, cut into small pieces

natural yoghurt, to serve (optional)

serves 4

Put the ginger ale, sugar and 3 tablespoons water in a large saucepan. Heat gently, stirring until the sugar has dissolved, then simmer for 2 minutes.

Add the rhubarb and poach it in the ginger syrup for about 10 minutes or until the fruit is tender. Remove from the heat and let cool before serving. If liked, stir a few tablespoons of the compote through some natural yoghurt, to serve.

COOK'S TIP
- Cooking the rhubarb in ginger ale helps to remove some of the tartness of the rhubarb. The cooking time will vary according to which type of rhubarb is used.

VARIATION
- **Rhubarb Fool** Cook the rhubarb as above, then drain off any excess cooking syrup. Transfer the rhubarb to a blender and process briefly. Stir into Home-made Custard (page 126), let cool and serve.

Did You Know?
Rhubarb is a good source of magnesium, which works with calcium to promote healthy bones, release energy and absorb other nutrients.

CHERRY COMPOTE

PREPARATION TIME
15 minutes
COOKING TIME 20 minutes

500 g unblemished cherries

50 g caster sugar

serves 4

Remove the stones from the cherries. Do this over a bowl so you can catch the juice.

Put the cherries and any juice in a heavy based saucepan. Add the sugar and simmer gently, stirring occasionally, until the sugar has dissolved. Simmer for a further 5–8 minutes or until the fruit is tender. Using a slotted draining spoon, remove the cherries from the liquid and transfer them to a serving bowl.

Bring the cooking liquor to the boil, then simmer gently for 8–10 minutes or until reduced and slightly syrupy. Pour the sauce over the cherries and serve.

CHOCOLATE MOUSSE

Chocolate with a high cocoa solid content (at least 70 per cent) is a good source of antioxidants. It also contains iron and magnesium.

PREPARATION TIME 5–8 minutes, plus 1 hour chilling time

100 g plain chocolate (at least 70 per cent cocoa solids)

4 eggs, separated

1 teaspoon unsweetened cocoa powder

4 individual dishes or glasses, 150 g each

serves 4

Break the chocolate into small pieces and put them in a heatproof bowl. Place the bowl over a saucepan of gently simmering water (make sure the bottom of the bowl doesn't touch the water). Heat gently until melted. Remove the bowl from the heat and stir until smooth. Let cool.

Beat the eggs yolks into the cooled chocolate one at a time, beating well after each addition. Put the egg whites in a clean, grease-free bowl and whisk with a hand-held electric whisk until stiff peaks form. Using a large metal spoon, gently stir the egg whites into the chocolate mixture, taking care not to overmix and knock out the air.

Spoon the mixture into 4 individual dishes or glasses, then chill in the refrigerator for 1 hour. Sprinkle with a little cocoa powder and serve.

RASPBERRY MOUSSE

Not only is this pudding utterly delicious, it is packed with raspberries which are rich in vitamin C and are higher in folic acid and zinc than most other fruit.

PREPARATION TIME 12–15 minutes, plus 1 hour chilling time
COOKING TIME 10 minutes

225 g raspberries, plus extra to serve

4 tablespoons freshly squeezed orange juice

about 50 g caster sugar

300 ml double cream

2 egg whites

2 squares plain chocolate (at least 70 per cent cocoa solids), grated, to serve

4 individual dishes or glasses, 250 ml each

serves 4

Put the raspberries, orange juice and sugar, to taste, in a heavy based saucepan. Simmer gently for 10 minutes, stirring occasionally, until the fruit has collapsed and softened. Let cool slightly, then transfer to a blender and process to form a purée. If you would like a smooth result, push the purée through a fine non-metallic sieve. Let cool.

Whisk the cream until soft peaks form, then stir in the cooled raspberry purée. Put the egg whites in a clean, grease-free bowl and whisk with a hand-held electric whisk until stiff peaks form. Using a large metal spoon, gently stir the egg whites into the raspberry mixture taking care not to overmix and knock out the air.

Spoon the mousse into 4 individual dishes or glasses. Cover and chill in the refrigerator for at least 1 hour. Serve topped with extra raspberries and some grated chocolate.

COOK'S TIP
• You can omit the whisked egg whites from this recipe if you are serving it to somebody who should avoid uncooked eggs (page 4).

MARITIME MANGOES

One serving of this pudding contains one orange and half a mango, so it's packed with vitamin C to keep the immune system healthy.

PREPARATION TIME
15 minutes
FREEZING TIME 3 hours, plus
30 minutes softening time

4 large oranges

2 ripe mangoes

2 tablespoons finely grated
unwaxed orange zest

3 tablespoons low fat
natural yoghurt

3 tablespoons half fat
crème fraîche

2 squares plain chocolate (at
least 70 per cent cocoa solids),
grated, to serve (optional)

serves 4

Set the freezer to rapid freeze. Cut the oranges in half, scooping out the flesh and pith, taking care to leave the orange shells intact. If necessary, cut a small slice from the base of each orange shell to ensure they can stand upright.

Peel the mangoes and cut the flesh away from the stones. Chop the flesh into small pieces. Put the mango and orange flesh, orange zest, yoghurt and crème fraîche in a blender and process for 2–3 minutes until smooth.

Pour the mixture into a freezerproof container and freeze for 2 hours, stirring occasionally, to break up any ice crystals. Spoon the mixture into the orange shells, then freeze for 1 hour or until solid. Transfer the oranges to the refrigerator 30 minutes before serving to soften slightly. Top each one with a little grated chocolate, if using, and serve.

STRAWBERRY MOUNTAIN

Strawberries are rich in vitamin C and this pudding contains almost twice the recommended daily amount a child needs.

PREPARATION TIME
10–15 minutes
FREEZING TIME 1½–2 hours

900 g strawberries, hulled

150 g icing sugar, plus
1 tablespoon extra

freshly squeezed juice of
2 lemons

2 tablespoons double cream

serves 6–8

Put the strawberries in a blender or food processor and blend to form a purée. If you want a smoother result, push the purée through a non-metallic sieve to remove the pips. Transfer to a bowl and whisk in the icing sugar and lemon juice. Pour into a shallow, freezerproof container and freeze for 1½–2 hours until solid.

Meanwhile, put the cream and 1 tablespoon icing sugar in a small bowl and mix well. Cover and refrigerate.

Transfer the frozen strawberry mixture to the refrigerator 30 minutes before serving. When ready to serve, use a strong fork to scrape shreds of the frozen strawberries and divide them between 6 or 8 serving dishes. Top each serving with 1 teaspoon of the chilled cream and serve immediately.

COOK'S TIP
- Use a shallow, freezerproof container no deeper than 5 cm so that the mixture freezes quickly.

VARIATION
- Use raspberries, firm melons – such as Ogen or Galia – plums or oranges instead of the strawberries.

OATY APPLE CRUNCH

This pudding is packed with apples, oats and nuts, which all release their sugars slowly into the blood stream making it a real energy booster.

PREPARATION TIME 15 minutes
COOKING TIME 30–45 minutes

675 g cooking apples, peeled, cored and sliced

1 teaspoon ground cinnamon

40 g light muscovado sugar

Home-made Custard (see below), to serve

oat topping

175 g rolled oats

1 tablespoon wheatgerm

50 g mixed nuts, such as pecans, hazelnuts, almonds and walnuts, chopped or flaked

25 g sunflower seeds

25 g sesame seeds

2 tablespoons clear honey

2 tablespoons sunflower oil

a baking sheet

an ovenproof dish, 1.2 litres

serves 4–6

To make the oat topping, put the oats, wheatgerm, nuts and seeds in a heatproof bowl and mix well. Heat the honey and oil in a small saucepan over medium heat, stirring, until blended. Pour the honey mixture over the oats and stir until well coated. Spoon the mixture onto a baking sheet and bake in a preheated oven at 180°C (350°F) Gas 4 for 10–15 minutes or until the mixture is lightly toasted. Remove from the oven and let cool. (Once cold, the oat mixture can be store in an airtight container for up to 1 week).

Meanwhile, put the apples, cinnamon, sugar and 4 tablespoons water in a saucepan. Cover and heat gently, stirring occasionally, for 10–15 minutes until the apples have softened and the sugar has dissolved.

Transfer the apples to the ovenproof dish, sprinkle with the toasted oat mixture and press down lightly. Increase the oven temperature to 200°C (400°F) Gas 6 and bake in the oven for 10–15 minutes until bubbling. Serve with home-made custard.

COOK'S TIP
- Other fruits can be used instead of the apples. Try fresh apricots or plums, apples and blackberries or frozen summer berries, defrosted.

HOME-MADE CUSTARD

This mouthwatering custard takes only minutes to make and is free from the artificial thickeners, colourings, preservatives and sweeteners found in commercial versions.

PREPARATION TIME 5 minutes, plus 15 minutes infusing time
COOKING TIME 12–15 minutes

350 ml double cream

600 ml whole milk

1 vanilla pod

3 eggs

2 tablespoons caster sugar

makes 600 ml

Pour the cream and milk into a heavy based saucepan and add the vanilla pod. Heat gently until it reaches just below boiling point. Remove the pan from the heat, cover and let infuse for 15 minutes.

Whisk the eggs and caster sugar together, then gradually add the infused cream and milk, whisking constantly. Strain the mixture into a clean saucepan. Heat gently, whisking constantly, until the custard starts to thicken. Remove the pan from the heat and continue to whisk until the custard cools slightly and thickens. Pour into a jug and serve immediately.

VARIATIONS
- **Strawberry Custard** Blend 100 g ripe, hulled strawberries to a purée, then stir into the prepared custard, adding extra sugar, to taste, if necessary.
- **Banana Custard** Stir 1–2 ripe mashed bananas into the prepared custard.
- **Chocolate Custard** Stir 100 g melted plain chocolate (at least 70 per cent cocoa solids) into the prepared custard.

MIXED BERRY TARTLETS

If you haven't got the time to make the pastry yourself, just buy a large, ready-prepared pastry case and fill it with the crème fraîche and fruit.

PREPARATION TIME 20–25 minutes, plus 30 minutes chilling time
COOKING TIME 17 minutes

100 g plain flour, plus extra for dusting

100 g wholemeal flour

100 g unsalted butter, chilled and cut into small pieces

1 tablespoon finely grated unwaxed orange zest

for the filling

450 g mixed summer berries, including blueberries, strawberries and raspberries

300 ml half fat crème fraîche or natural yoghurt

1 tablespoon finely grated unwaxed orange zest

2 teaspoons icing sugar

a pastry cutter, 7.5 cm diameter

small bun tins

makes 12

To make the pastry, put the flours, butter and orange zest in a food processor and blend for 1–2 minutes until the mixture resembles breadcrumbs. With the machine running, gradually pour 3–4 tablespoons cold water through the feed tube until the mixture forms a ball.

Transfer the dough to a lightly floured work surface and knead until it is smooth and pliable. Wrap and chill in the refrigerator for 30 minutes.

Roll out the pastry thinly on a lightly floured work surface. Using the pastry cutter, cut out 12 rounds and line the bun tin with them. Prick the bases lightly with a fork, then put a small piece of crumbled foil in each one.

Bake in a preheated oven at 200°C (400°F) Gas 6 for 12 minutes. Remove the foil and return the pastry cases to the oven for a further 3–5 minutes until the pastry is cooked. Remove from the oven and let cool before filling.

To prepare the filling, hull the strawberries and raspberries, if necessary, and cut any large fruit in half. Put the crème fraîche or yoghurt and orange zest in a bowl and mix. Spoon it into the cold pastry cases and put the fruit on top. Sprinkle with a little icing sugar and serve immediately.

COOK'S TIP
- To save time, you can make double the amount of pastry given here and wrap, label and freeze the extra quantity. Use within 1 month. Defrost thoroughly in the refrigerator before using.

Did You Know?

Berries are nature's powerhouse fruit. They taste great and are densely packed with antioxidants, phytochemicals and flavonoids. They are also high in fibre and vitamin C, and relatively low in sugar. Blueberries contain more antioxidants than other fruit so don't just add them to puddings, add them to yoghurt, breakfast cereals or eat them just as they are!

PARTY FOOD

Why is it that when it comes to birthdays, we parents think it is perfectly acceptable to feed our children – and all their friends – obscene amounts of sugar, fat and salt along with a cocktail of artificial colourings, flavourings and preservatives?

Synthetic, sugar laden fizzy drinks, crisps and snacks packed with saturated fat and salt, cheap white bread sandwiches filled with high fat fillings, sausages made from the cheapest offcuts of meat and commercially prepared birthday cakes decorated with sometimes as many as five separate colourings (many of which have been shown to cause behavioural problems in up to 25 per cent of all small children) have all come to be accepted as normal birthday party fayre. Given that most children experience huge sugar rushes after eating these foods, it's no wonder that most children's parties have a tendency to disintegrate into utter chaos.

However, the good news is that it's perfectly simple to create birthday party feasts that your children will genuinely love and that are good for them. In this chapter you'll find a collection of recipes designed to inspire you to prepare a really healthy (and delicious) celebratory feast, many of which can be used at any time, not just for parties. Equally, there are lots of ideas throughout the rest of the book that would make a welcome party-time treat (see list, far right).

DRINKS

Commercially prepared fizzy drinks are very high in sugar and additives. So instead, serve sparkling mineral water mixed with fresh fruit juice or a little low sugar cordial. For lots more healthy drink ideas, see pages 42, 68 and 71.

PARTY BAGS

If you want to provide a party bag for each child to take home, avoid filling them with sugar- and additive-laden sweets. Instead, choose non-food items like stickers, mini crayons, balloons or bubble blowing kits.

REAL ALTERNATIVES

Honey-glazed top-quality, high meat content organic sausages on cocktail sticks • cherry tomatoes and cheese cubes on cocktail sticks • fruit platter, including grapes, melon slices, strawberries, clementines and kiwi fruit • chocolate crunchies – whole bran cereal and sultanas stirred into melted chocolate and served in paper cake cases • any of the sandwich suggestions from page 55, cut into small pieces or shaped with a pastry cutter • bowls of dried fruit, such as cherries, raisins, sultanas and apricots • digestive biscuits or oatcakes topped with cream cheese and halved grapes • hot dogs made from top-quality, high meat content organic sausages, served in wholemeal rolls with fresh Salsa (page 96) or Real Tomato Ketchup (page 105) • thick slices of organic ham spread with cream cheese, rolled up and secured with a cocktail stick

PRESENTATION

Children are even more easily swayed by the look of food than adults. Therefore, the key to ensuring your healthy, wholesome spread is met with as much enthusiasm as the usual array of junk food that is on offer at parties is to focus on presentation. Cut sandwiches into fun shapes using biscuit cutters; make faces on mini pizzas using vegetables; chop up brightly coloured fruit and arrange it on the table; pile the hazelnut brownies into a pyramid; and make best use of all the usual themed tablecloths, paper plates, hats and streamers.

PARTY FOOD IDEAS FROM THE REST OF THE BOOK

Apricot and Walnut Flapjacks (page 60) cut into bite-sized pieces • Double Chocolate and Hazelnut Brownies (page 64) cut into bite-sized squares • Gingerbread People (page 63) • Ice Cream (page 117) – why not create a home-made ice cream parlour with different flavoured ice creams and lots of different toppings and sauces? • a selection of dips (pages 48–51) served with toasted pita bread strips, Bread Sticks, crunchy Vegetable Sticks (page 48) and Roasted Root Vegetable Dippers (page 51) • Coleslaw (page 59) • Tuna Pasta Salad (page 56) • Couscous Salad (page 56) • Oaty Chocolate Crunchies (page 60) • Sweet Potato Chips (page 90) • Oven-baked Wedges (page 102) • Vegetable Crisps (page 46) • Home-made Sausages with Real Tomato Ketchup (page 105)

SMOKED SALMON TORTILLA WHEELS

Over recent years, the excessive use of chemicals, antibiotics, artificial colourings and growth promoters in farmed salmon has given rise to a variety of health concerns. Where possible, buy wild or organically farmed salmon.

PREPARATION TIME
15 minutes

4 small flour tortillas

4 tablespoons half fat cream cheese

1 teaspoon finely grated unwaxed lemon zest

1 tablespoon freshly snipped chives

200 g thinly sliced smoked salmon

1 tablespoon freshly squeezed lemon juice

freshly ground black pepper (optional)

to serve (optional)

cherry tomatoes

salad leaves

lemon wedges

cocktail sticks

makes 32

Wrap the tortillas in foil and heat in a preheated oven at 180°C (350°F) Gas 4 for 10 minutes, or according to the instructions on the packet. Leave to cool.

Meanwhile, put the cream cheese, lemon zest and chives in a bowl and beat with a wooden spoon until softened.

Spread 1 tablespoon of the cream cheese mixture over each tortilla and top with some thinly sliced smoked salmon. Sprinkle with a little lemon juice and grind over some black pepper, if using. Roll up tightly and secure with cocktail sticks. If not using immediately, wrap in damp greaseproof paper and store in the refrigerator for up to 3 hours until required.

To serve, cut into small slices and discard the cocktail sticks. Arrange the tortilla wheels on a serving plate and put some cherry tomatoes, salad leaves and lemon wedges, if using, around the plate.

COOK'S TIP
- The tortilla wheels can be frozen before cutting into slices as long as the salmon hasn't been previously frozen. Wrap well, label and freeze for up to 1 month. To serve, defrost thoroughly in the refrigerator, then cut into thin slices.

VARIATIONS
- Replace the cream cheese and smoked salmon with Smoked Trout Pâté (page 52).
- Use cream cheese mixed with a small amount of tomato purée and some thinly sliced ham.
- Spread Guacamole (page 51) over the tortillas and top with thin strips of red and yellow peppers or blanched baby asparagus spears. Roll up and secure as above. Leave in the refrigerator for at least 15 minutes before cutting into wheels.

Did You Know?

I have seen this recipe made using wholemeal bread instead of tortillas. This would be okay, but tortillas have a much lower rating on the glycaemic index (approximately half that of wholemeal bread) so they provide a far steadier, more sustained rise in blood sugar levels.

HONEY GLAZED CHICKEN DRUMSTICKS

What could be more nutritious, simple or delicious than these honey-glazed chicken drumsticks?

PREPARATION TIME
5 minutes
COOKING TIME 25 minutes

12 chicken drumsticks,
about 100 g each

6 tablespoons clear honey

serves 4

Lightly rinse the chicken drumsticks, removing the skin, if preferred. Put them in a roasting tin with 4 tablespoons water. Bake in a preheated oven at 190°C (375°F) Gas 5 for 5 minutes, turning them over halfway through.

Remove the tin from the oven and drizzle over the honey. Return to the oven and continue to cook for 15–20 minutes, basting occasionally with the honey and juices in the tin, until golden brown, sticky and thoroughly cooked. To check, pierce the thickest part of the drumstick with a skewer; the juices should run clear. If there is any sign of blood, continue to cook for a few minutes more. If in doubt, cut through one of the drumsticks to the bone to check.

Remove the chicken from the oven and drain well before serving.

MINI BREADED MEATBALLS

I can guarantee that these home-made meatballs, served with oven-baked wedges, will go down a treat at a children's party.

PREPARATION TIME
12–15 minutes, plus 30 minutes
chilling time
COOKING TIME 12–15 minutes

1–2 slices day-old
wholemeal bread

1 recipe Beef Burgers
(page 106)

1 tablespoon wholemeal flour

1 large egg, beaten

to serve

Salsa (page 96)

mayonnaise

low fat fromage frais mixed with
chopped fresh herbs

20 cocktail sticks

makes 20 balls

Cut the bread into small strips. Put them in a blender or food processor and blend briefly to make breadcrumbs. Transfer to a shallow dish.

Prepare the Beef Burger mixture as directed on page 106. Use clean hands to shape the mixture into about 20 even balls about the size of an apricot (a perfect job for little hands).

Put the flour on a plate and the beaten egg in a shallow dish. Roll the balls in the flour until well coated, then dip them in the egg, shaking off any excess. Roll them in the breadcrumbs until evenly coated and transfer to a large plate. Cover and chill in the refrigerator for at least 30 minutes.

Put the meatballs in a non-stick roasting tin and cook in a preheated oven at 200°C (400°F) Gas 6 for 12–15 minutes, turning the balls occasionally, until golden brown and crisp.

Put a cocktail stick in each meatball and transfer to a large serving plate. Serve warm, accompanied by dipping sauces, such as salsa, mayonnaise or herby fromage frais.

COOK'S TIP
• These balls would make a great pasta dish. Prepare the Tomato Sauce for Pasta (page 86), add the meatballs to the sauce and heat thoroughly. Serve on top of freshly cooked, hot pasta.

FAIRY CAKES

Shop-bought fairy cakes are a mixture of white flour, saturated fat, sugar and coloured icing, which may contain additives known to cause behavioural problems. These avoid unnecessary additives by using white icing and naturally coloured cherries and the sugar content is kept low by adding orange juice.

PREPARATION TIME 15 minutes
COOKING TIME 15–20 minutes

75 g self-raising flour

75 g wholemeal self-raising flour

1 teaspoon baking powder

100 g golden caster sugar

100 ml sunflower oil

2 eggs, beaten

4 tablespoons freshly squeezed orange juice

200 g golden icing sugar

naturally coloured glacé cherries, to decorate

a 12-hole bun tin, lined with 12 paper cases

makes 12

Sift the flours and baking powder into a large bowl and stir in the sugar. Using a wooden spoon or hand-held electric mixer, gradually beat in the oil and then the eggs until the mixture is smooth and creamy. Add 1 tablespoon orange juice and mix gently to give a soft, dropping consistency. Add a little more orange juice if the mixture feels too stiff.

Spoon the mixture into the paper cases, filling them about three-quarters full. Bake in a preheated oven at 180°C (350°F) Gas 4 for 15–20 minutes until golden and firm to the touch. Remove from the oven and let cool.

Sift the icing sugar into a bowl. Add the remaining orange juice and mix until smooth. Spoon over the tops of the cooled cakes. Let set slightly, then decorate with the cherries. Best eaten within 2 days.

VARIATION
• Instead of the cherries, use good quality grated chocolate to decorate.

DOUBLE CHOCOLATE FRUITY SQUARES

PREPARATION TIME 15 minutes, plus 2 hours chilling time

200 g plain chocolate (at least 70 per cent cocoa solids)

100 g sunflower margarine

2 tablespoons freshly squeezed orange juice

150 g low fat digestive biscuits

60 g good quality white chocolate

50 g raisins

75 g ready-to-eat dried apricots, chopped

50 g dried cherries or cranberries

a baking tin, 18 cm square, lightly greased

makes 16 squares

Break the plain chocolate into small squares and put them in a heavy based saucepan. Add the margarine and orange juice and heat gently for 3–4 minutes, stirring occasionally, until melted. Stir until smooth.

Crush the biscuits in a food processor or put them in a polythene bag and crush with a rolling pin. Roughly chop the white chocolate. Add the crushed biscuits, white chocolate and all the dried fruit to the melted chocolate mixture. Stir well so all the ingredients are lightly coated with chocolate.

Spoon into the prepared tin and press down lightly with the back of a wooden spoon. Transfer to the refrigerator and let set for at least 2 hours. Cut into squares, to serve. Store lightly covered in the refrigerator for up to 4 days.

VARIATION
• Replace this selection of dried fruit with others of your choice, such as sultanas or mango, and add some finely chopped nuts if you like.

CHOCOLATE-DIPPED FRUIT

There is nothing wrong with letting your children eat chocolate from time to time, especially if it is used to coat fresh fruit as it is here. Kids will love helping to make these.

PREPARATION TIME 10–15 minutes, plus 1 hour setting time

500 g fresh, ripe, but firm fruit, such as strawberries, apples, seedless grapes, physalis or satsumas

100 g plain chocolate (at least 70 per cent cocoa solids), broken into pieces

1 teaspoon golden syrup

a few cocktail sticks or skewers

serves 4

Wash the fruit and dry it carefully with kitchen paper. Leave the small fruit whole. Cut the apples into thin wedges and remove the core. Divide the satsumas into segments.

Put the chocolate and golden syrup in a heatproof bowl. Place the bowl over a saucepan of gently simmering water, making sure the base of the bowl doesn't come into contact with the water. Heat gently, stirring occasionally, until the chocolate is melted and smooth. Remove the bowl from the heat and let cool slightly.

Pierce a piece of fruit with a cocktail stick or skewer and dip it into the melted chocolate. Transfer to a sheet of non-stick baking parchment and leave to set for about 1 hour. Eat within 3–4 hours of coating.

ICED LOLLIES

These lollies are a real summer treat for kids and they are full of fresh fruit or freshly squeezed fruit juice.

PREPARATION TIME 5–10 minutes
FREEZING TIME 2–3 hours

600 ml freshly squeezed fruit juice, such as orange, apple or pineapple juice or 450 g fresh ripe fruit, such as strawberries, raspberries or a mixture of both

40–50 g golden caster sugar (optional)

8 iced lolly moulds, 80 ml each

makes 8 lollies

Set the freezer to rapid freeze. Rinse out the iced lolly moulds with cold water and put them in their rack.

If using fruit juice, carefully pour the juice into the moulds, then push the handle tops into the lollies.

If using fresh ripe fruit, remove any stalks, rinse lightly and cut any large fruit in half. Put the fruit in a saucepan, add sugar to taste and 150 ml water. Cook over gentle heat for 5 minutes or until the fruit has collapsed. Let cool slightly, then transfer to a food processor or blender and process to form a purée. Push the purée through a fine, non-metallic sieve to remove the pips.

Make the purée up to 600 ml with filtered water or freshly squeezed orange juice. Pour it into the iced lolly moulds, then push a handle top into each lolly.

Freeze for at least 4 hours until frozen. Use within 2–3 days.

VARIATION
• Fill the lolly moulds with milkshake (page 71) or one of the smoothies on page 42, and freeze as above.

CHOCOLATE & RASPBERRY BIRTHDAY CAKE

Although this recipe contains cream (or half fat crème fraîche), it doesn't require the butter used in most cakes. The highly refined white flour is also absent and instead it uses protein-packed almonds.

PREPARATION TIME 20 minutes
COOKING TIME 25–30 minutes

4 eggs

150 g golden caster sugar

100 g plain chocolate (at least 70 per cent cocoa solids), broken into small pieces

150 g ground almonds

150 ml double cream or half fat crème fraîche

200–300 g fresh raspberries

2 sandwich tins, 18 cm diameter, lightly greased and base-lined with baking parchment

serves 8

Put the eggs and sugar in a heatproof bowl and place over a saucepan of gently simmering water. Whisk with a hand-held electric mixer for 5–8 minutes until very thick and creamy. The mixture should leave a trail when it drips from the whisk. Remove the bowl from the saucepan and whisk for 3–5 minutes until cool.

Put the chocolate in a small heatproof bowl and place over a saucepan of gently simmering water, making sure that the base of the bowl doesn't come into contact with the water. Heat gently until the chocolate has melted. Remove the bowl from the saucepan and stir the chocolate until smooth. Let cool.

Gradually add the cooled chocolate to the whisked egg mixture, stirring gently. Stir in the ground almonds, mixing lightly. Divide the mixture evenly between the 2 sandwich tins, tap each tin lightly on the work surface to remove any air bubbles.

Bake in a preheated oven at 180°C (350°F) Gas 4 for 25–30 minutes until well risen and the tops spring back when touched lightly with your finger. Remove the cakes from the oven and let cool in the tins for about 10 minutes before transferring them to a wire cooling rack to cool completely. The surface will crisp up and crack as it cools. Remove and discard the baking parchment.

Whisk the cream, if using, with a hand-held electric mixer until soft peaks form. Spread half the cream or crème fraîche over one layer of the cake and top with half the raspberries. Put the second cake layer on top and decorate with the remaining cream or crème fraîche and raspberries. Store lightly covered in the refrigerator until required. The undecorated cake will keep for 2 days.

VARIATION

- For an alternative birthday cake idea, make the Easy Carrot Cake Cups on page 64. Put a slice of banana on top of each one (held in place with some lemon cream cheese icing) to act as a birthday candle holder, then carefully stack the cakes pyramid-style on a plate. Light the candles when ready. This works particularly well for younger children because each child can have their own cake and get a chance to blow out the candles. They are easy to put in party bags, too.

INDEX

A

additives, 8, 17–18

allergies, 25

apples: apple and carrot juice, 68

apple and oat muffins, 36

apple tea bread, 67

coleslaw, 59

home-made sausages, 105

honey, apple and banana shake, 71

oaty apple crunch, 126

apricots: apricot and walnut

flapjack, 60

sticky toffee and apricot sauce, 118

avocados: chicken and avocado

roll, 55

guacamole, 51

B

bagel, smoked salmon and cream

cheese, 55

baked beans, home-made 72, 76

baked sweet potatoes with cheesy

lentil hash and crispy bacon, 85

bananas: banana custard, 126

honey, apple and banana shake, 71

sesame street, 42

beans: baked beans, home-made,

72, 76

chicken and vegetable faijitas, 96

Tuscan tuna and bean sauce, 89

beef: beef burgers, 106

mini breaded meatballs, 135

ragù, 86

biscuits: chocolate chip and oatmeal

biscuits, 63

gingerbread people, 63

bread: bread sticks, 48

easy peasy wholemeal bread, 38

hoummus pita pockets, 55

sardine bruschetta, 76

breakfast bars, 32

broccoli: broccoli cheese, 113

broccoli pesto, 86

creamy potato and broccoli soup, 74

brownies, 64

bruschetta, sardine, 76

burgers, 72, 106–9

C

cabbage: coleslaw, 59

shredded spring cabbage and

ham, 113

cakes: chocolate and raspberry

birthday cake, 140

date bars, 67

double chocolate and hazelnut

brownies, 64

double chocolate fruity squares, 136

easy carrot cake cups, 64

fairy cakes, 136

calcium, 12, 13

carbohydrates, 10–11

carrots: apple and carrot juice, 68

easy carrot cake cups, 64

honey glazed carrots, 94

cereals, breakfast, 30

cheese: baked sweet potatoes with

cheesy lentil hash and crispy

bacon, 85

broccoli cheese, 113

cheese and spinach soufflés, 79

smoked salmon and cream cheese

bagel, 55

cherry compote, 121

chickpeas: hoummus, 51

chicken: chicken and avocado

roll, 55

chicken and pea risotto, 98

chicken and vegetable faijitas, 96

chicken burgers, 106

chicken nuggets, 72, 102

honey glazed chicken drumsticks,

135

ready, steady, go stir fry, 101

chips, 72

chocolate, 60

chocolate and raspberry birthday

cake, 140

chocolate chip and oatmeal

biscuits, 63

chocolate custard, 126

chocolate-dipped fruit, 139

chocolate ice cream, 117

chocolate monkey milkshake, 71

chocolate mousse, 122

double chocolate and hazelnut

brownies, 64

double chocolate fruity squares, 136

oaty chocolate crunchies, 60

cod: fish cakes, 93

fish fingers, 90

fish pie, 94

saffron fish pilaff, 59

coleslaw, 59

colourings, 8, 17–18

cooking, 25

couscous salad, 56

crisps, vegetable, 46

crunchy dip, 48

custard, 114, 126

D

date bars, 67

dippy eggs, 41

dips, 48–51

dried fruit: breakfast bars, 32

double chocolate fruity squares, 136

muesli, 32

drinks, 45

fresh fruit drinks, 68

milkshakes, 71

party drinks, 130

smoothies, 42

E

eggs, 25

dippy eggs, 41

frittata, 79

ham omelette, 41

poached eggs, 41

scrambled eggs, 41

essential fatty acids, 12

F

fairy cakes, 136

fajitas, chicken and vegetable, 96

fats, 8, 17

fillers, processed foods, 17

fish cakes, 93

fish fingers, 72, 90

fish pie, 94

flapjack, apricot and walnut, 60

flavourings, 8, 18

food labels, 25

frittata, 79

fruit, 8, 11

chocolate-dipped fruit, 139

compotes, 121

full of fruit smoothie, 42

ice cream, 117

iced lollies, 139

mixed berry tartlets, 129

servings, 13

summer berry breakfast, 42

full of fruit smoothie, 42

G

garlic dip, creamy, 48

get up 'n' go smoothie, 42

gingerbread people, 63

grains, 10, 13

granola, 32

green beans, lemony, 93

guacamole, 51

H

ham: ham omelette, 41

shredded spring cabbage and

ham, 113

hazelnuts: crunchy dip, 48

double chocolate and hazelnut

brownies, 64

vegetable and nut pâté, 52

honey, 25

honey, apple and banana shake, 71
honey roasted nuts and seeds, 46
hoummus, 51
    hoummus pita pockets, 55
hydrogenated fats, 17

I

ice cream, 114
    knickerbocker glory, 118
    vanilla ice cream, 117
iced lollies, 139
ingredients, 26–7

J

jelly, 114

K

ketchup, real tomato, 105
knickerbocker glory, 118

L

lamb: mini shepherd's pies with four
    veg mash, 110
lemon cordial, 68
lentils: baked sweet potatoes with
    cheesy lentil hash, 85
lollies, iced, 139

M

mackerel: fish pie, 94
mangoes, maritime, 125
mealtimes, 20–2
meat, mechanically recovered, 17
meatballs, mini breaded, 135
melon: sesame street, 42
milk: milkshakes, 71
    smoothies, 42
mousses, 114, 122
muesli, 32
muffins, apple and oat, 36

N

noodles: ready, steady, go stir fry, 101
nutrition, 10–19
nuts: allergies, 25
    honey roasted nuts and seeds, 46
    nut burgers, 109

O

oats: apple and oat muffins, 36
    apricot and walnut flapjack, 60
    breakfast bars, 32

chocolate chip and oatmeal
    biscuits, 63
date bars, 67
muesli, 32
oaty apple crunch, 126
oaty chocolate crunchies, 60
overnight oats, 35
pink porridge, 35
omega fats, 12, 52
omelette, ham, 41
oranges: maritime mangoes, 125
organic foods, 19

P

pasta: roasted vegetable sauce, 89
    tomato sauce for pasta, 86
    tuna pasta salad, 56
    Tuscan tuna and bean sauce, 89
    walnut pesto, 86
pâtés: smoked trout pâté, 52
    vegetable and nut pâté, 52
pear and ginger juice, 68
peas: chicken and pea risotto, 98
    fish fingers with sweet potato chips
    and pea purée, 90
peppers: couscous salad, 56
    ready, steady, go stir fry, 101
pesticides, 18
pesto, walnut, 86
pilaff, saffron fish, 59
pita pockets, hoummus, 55
pizza, 72, 82
pork: home-made sausages, 105
porridge, pink, 35
potatoes, 10, 13
    chips, 72
    creamy potato and broccoli
    soup, 74
    fish cakes, 93
    fish pie, 94
    oven-baked wedges, 102
    warm potato salad, 85
preservatives, 18
protein, 12, 13
puddings, 114–29
pumpkin soup, 74

Q

quiche, simple vegetable, 80

R

raspberries: chocolate and raspberry
    birthday cake, 140
    knickerbocker glory, 118
    raspberry milkshake, 71
    raspberry mousse, 122
    raspberry ripple ice cream, 117
    sesame street, 42
ready meals, 9, 72
ready, steady, go stir fry, 101
refusing food, 23
rhubarb compote, 121
rice: chicken and pea risotto, 98
    saffron fish pilaff, 59

S

saffron fish pilaff, 59
salads, 56–9
    coleslaw, 59
    couscous salad, 56
    saffron fish pilaff, 59
    tuna pasta salad, 56
    warm potato salad, 85
salt, 8, 14
sardine bruschetta, 76
saturated fat, 8, 17
sauces: roasted vegetable sauce, 89
    sticky toffee and apricot sauce, 118
    strawberry sauce, 118
    tomato sauce for pasta, 86
sausages, 72, 105
seeds, honey roasted nuts and, 46
sesame seeds: crunchy dip, 48
    sesame street, 42
    sesame sugar snap peas, 113
shepherd's pies with four veg mash, 110
smoked haddock: saffron fish
    pilaff, 59
smoked salmon: smoked salmon and
    cream cheese bagel, 55
    smoked salmon tortilla wheels, 133
smoked trout pâté, 52
smoothies, 42
soufflés, cheese and spinach, 79
soups, 74
spinach: cheese and spinach
    soufflés, 79
    creamy spinach, 113
    fish pie, 94

sticky toffee and apricot sauce, 118
strawberries: pink porridge, 35
    strawberry custard, 126
    strawberry mountain, 125
    strawberry sauce, 118
sugar, 8, 14–15
sugar snap peas, sesame, 113
summer berry breakfast, 42
sweet potatoes: baked sweet
    potatoes, 85
    sweet potato chips, 90
sweeteners, artificial, 18

T

tartlets, mixed berry, 129
tea bread, apple, 67
tomatoes: couscous salad, 56
    real tomato ketchup, 105
    tomato sauce for pasta, 86
    Tuscan tuna and bean sauce, 89
tortillas: chicken and vegetable
    faijitas, 96
    smoked salmon tortilla wheels, 133
tuna: tuna pasta salad, 56
    Tuscan tuna and bean sauce, 89

V

vanilla ice cream, 117
vegetables, 8, 11
    chicken and vegetable faijitas, 96
    dippers, 48
    mini shepherd's pies with four veg
    mash, 110
    roasted root dippers, 51
    roasted vegetable sauce, 89
    servings, 13
    simple vegetable quiche, 80
    vegetable and nut pâté, 52
    vegetable burgers, 109
    vegetable crisps, 46
vitamins, 12

W

walnut pesto, 86
wholemeal bread, easy peasy, 38

Y

yoghurt, 30, 114
    knickerbocker glory, 118
    milkshakes, 71
    summer berry breakfast, 42

author's acknowledgments

My biggest thank you has to go to my two adorable little boys, Barney and Brook, not only for inspiring me to write this book in the first place, but for reminding me on a daily basis just how important it is to serve our next generation the very best food we possibly can. Thanks also to Louis, for being the best husband and dad (ever!). Last, but by no means least, I'd like to thank all of the brilliant team at Ryland Peters & Small, especially Sharon Cochrane and Alison Starling, and Gina Steer.

FEEDBACK

If you have any feedback about any of the recipes or issues in this book, or if you require further information about healthy eating for kids, please visit www.realfoodforkids.com or email me at r.a.hill@realfoodforkids.com.

publisher's acknowledgments

The publisher would like to thank the adorable models, Christina, Darla, Ellie, Elliot, Eve, Gaia, Georgina, Gregory, Hassia, Havana, Sammy and Thomas. A special thank you also goes to their parents.